D0623534

The Christian Family Easter Book

EDITED BY

Ron & Lyn Klug

Augsburg Publishing House
Minneapolis

THE CHRISTIAN FAMILY EASTER BOOK

Copyright © 1989 Augsburg Publishing House

Illustrated by Jack Norman

Library of Congress Cataloging-in-Publication Data

THE CHRISTIAN FAMILY EASTER BOOK.

  Summary: Includes stories, lore, poems,
prayers, and songs to celebrate the true
meaning of Easter.
  1. Easter—Literary collections.
[1. Easter—Literary collections] I. Klug,
Ron. II. Klug, Lyn.
PZ5.C463   1989   [Fic]   88-34976
ISBN 0-8066-2395-0

Manufactured in the U.S.A.   APH 10-1114

1   2   3   4   5   6   7   8   9   0   1   2   3   4   5   6   7   8   9

Contents

Introduction

For Christians, Easter means that Christ is risen, victorious over sin and death. Easter means that Jesus is alive, with us always, an unfailing source of strength and comfort. Easter means new life and joy and power to follow Christ in lives of love and service.

How do we begin to communicate this to our children and grandchildren? One way is by reading aloud stories, poems, and prayers that relate the importance of Easter.

The Christian Family Easter Book contains 40 stories, beginning with a retelling of the story of Jesus' death and resurrection as we find it in the Bible. There are also articles and stories that explain some of the customs and symbols associated with Easter around the world. Other stories are about the joys and problems connected with a family's celebration of Easter. And some stories are just for fun.

In many parts of the world, Easter is observed in spring. As the earth comes to life again, we are reminded of Jesus' resurrection and the new life he brings. So some of the stories are concerned with children's reactions to spring. Other stories illustrate the new life to which Jesus calls us, as we see children learning to forgive, reaching out to others, and helping those in need.

All the stories can be read to preschoolers and children in the early elementary grades. By second or third grade many children will be able to read them for themselves.

We have also chosen poems for Easter and spring, a group of prayers, and some songs especially appropriate for this time of year.

As in our earlier anthologies, *The Christian Family Bedtime Reading Book* and *The Christian Family Christmas Book,* we suggest that you may want to try a simple family ritual. Begin with a story or two. Then read one or more poems, sing a song or read the words, and end with a prayer.

Jesus has promised, "Where two or three come together in my name, there am I with them" (Matthew 18:20). Our prayer is that you and the children you love will experience that presence and grow in the new life God has given us in Christ.

The Story of Easter   Retold by Ron and Lyn Klug

Jesus loved people and helped them in many ways. He healed people who were sick. He fed those who were hungry. He told people how much God loved them. Many people loved Jesus and wanted to be near him.

Once Jesus came to Jerusalem for a special religious holiday. He rode a donkey through the crowded streets. People waved palm branches and shouted "Hosanna! Blessed is the one God has sent to save us. Hosanna in the highest!"

Some of the religious leaders were jealous because the people were following Jesus. They decided to try to get rid of Jesus. They talked to one of Jesus' friends, a man named Judas, and promised him 30 pieces of silver if he would help them capture Jesus. And Judas agreed.

On the day some people call Maundy Thursday, Jesus told his disciples to find a quiet room where they could have a special meal called the Passover. This meal celebrated the time when God freed the Jewish people from slavery in Egypt.

Before the meal Jesus brought in a pan of water and a towel. He began to wash the feet of his disciples. Usually this was done only by a slave. When he finished, Jesus said, "From now on, I want you to serve one another the way I served you."

While they were eating the Passover meal, Jesus took some bread and gave a piece to each disciple, saying, "Take and eat. This is my body given for you. Do this to remember me."

Then he gave each one a drink of wine and said, "This is my blood which will be shed for you for the forgiveness of sins. Do this to remember me."

Since then Christians all over the world share bread and wine in this way and remember Jesus in the Lord's Supper or Holy Communion.

After Jesus and his disciples sang some songs, they walked to a park outside Jerusalem called the Garden of Gethsemane. While his friends waited in the darkness, Jesus prayed, "Father, I am afraid of what is going to happen. But I want to do whatever you want me to do."

Suddenly out of the darkness came a crowd of men with sticks and torches. In the front was Judas, who led them to Jesus. All of Jesus' disciples were afraid and ran off, leaving Jesus alone with his enemies.

The mob took Jesus to the high priest's house for a trial, even though it was the middle of the night. The high priest brought in witnesses who told lies about Jesus. Finally the high priest asked Jesus, "Are you the Son of God?"

Jesus said, "I am."

The Jewish leaders were so angry that they decided Jesus should die. They took him to the Roman governor, Pontius Pilate, to be sentenced to death.

But Pilate did not think Jesus deserved to die. He wanted to release Jesus. It was a custom that one prisoner could be set free at Passover time. But the people said, "Give us Barabbas, instead." Barabbas was a bad man, but Pilate finally agreed. Barabbas was set free and Jesus was led away to die.

On the day we call Good Friday soldiers made Jesus carry a heavy cross to a hill named Golgotha. There they nailed Jesus to a cross, and there Jesus died.

One of Jesus' friends named Joseph of Arimathea did something that was very brave. He went to the governor and asked if he could bury Jesus' body. When he was given permission, Joseph and another man who loved Jesus took his body and put it in a cave that had been cut out of solid rock. They began preparing Jesus' body for burial, but because it was now Friday evening, the beginning of the Jewish Sabbath when no one was allowed to work, they had to wait until Sunday morning to finish. They rolled a stone in front of the tomb and left.

Early on Sunday morning while it was still dark, Mary Magdalene, a friend of Jesus, went to the tomb. When she came to the place where Jesus had been laid, she saw that the stone was already rolled away from the entrance. Mary ran back to the city and told Peter and another of Jesus' disciples, "Someone has taken Jesus' body out of the tomb, and I don't know where they have put him!"

When they heard the news, the two of them, Peter and John, decided to see for themselves. They ran as fast as they could to Jesus' tomb. John ran faster so he reached the tomb first, but he stood outside waiting. Peter came and ran right in. He saw the cloths Jesus' body had been wrapped in, but Jesus was not there. The disciples sadly went back to their homes.

But Mary Magdalene stood outside the tomb, crying. As she cried, she bent down and looked in the tomb. There she saw two angels dressed in white. "Why are you crying?" they asked.

"Someone has taken my Lord away, and I don't know where they have put him," said Mary Magdalene.

As she spoke, a man came up and stood near her. "Why are you crying?" he asked.

Mary turned around and, thinking he was the gardener who was in charge of the tomb, she said, "If you have taken my Lord's body, please tell me where you have put him."

Softly, the man said her name, "Mary."

Then Mary recognized the man. It was Jesus. He was alive!

Later two of Jesus' friends were walking down a road to a town called Emmaus. As they walked, they were talking about Jesus' death, and they were very discouraged.

A third man began to walk along with them. He asked them why they were sad.

"We believed that Jesus was the Savior, and now he's dead," they said.

The third man walked with them a while and explained why the Savior had to die.

When they came near Emmaus, the two men were so interested in what the stranger was saying that they invited him to stay overnight with them.

As they sat down to eat, the stranger took a loaf of bread and broke off a piece for each of them. At that moment they realized that the man was Jesus.

Jesus also came to a group of his disciples who were hiding in a room, afraid of Jesus' enemies. "Don't be afraid," Jesus said. "I am alive, and I am here with you."

One of the disciples, named Thomas, was not there. When the others told him they had seen Jesus, he did not believe them. To this day he is called "doubting Thomas." He said, "Unless I see Jesus myself and touch the nail marks in his hands, I won't believe that he is alive."

One night Jesus came to the disciples when Thomas was there. Jesus said, "Touch me and see that I am really alive."

Thomas did this, and he believed.

Jesus said, "Happy are those who have not seen me, but have believed in me anyway."

Once some of the disciples were fishing all night without catching even one fish. Early in the morning they saw a man on the shore who called to them, "Throw your net out on the other side of the boat."

They threw their net out, and soon it was so full of fish that it was about to break.

"That must be Jesus!" Peter said. He jumped into the water and swam to Jesus. The other disciples rowed to shore, dragging the net full of fish.

Jesus had made a fire on the beach, and there he and the disciples had breakfast together.

For 40 days after his death, Jesus appeared to those who believed in him. Then he called them together and said, "Now it is time for me to return to God. Go and teach all people everywhere about God's love. Baptize them, and teach them to live the way I have showed you. I will be with you always, even to the end of the world."

An Easter Carol

Christina Georgina Rossetti

Spring bursts today,
*   For Christ is risen and all the earth's at play.*

Flash forth, thou Sun,
*   The rain is over and gone, its work is done.*

Winter is past,
*   Sweet Spring is come at last, is come at last.*

Bud, Fig and Vine,
*   Bud, Olive, fat with fruit and oil and wine.*

Break forth this morn
*   In roses, thou but yesterday a thorn.*

Uplift thy head,
*   O pure white Lily through the Winter dead.*

Beside your dams
*   Leap and rejoice, you merry making Lambs.*

All Herds and Flocks
*   Rejoice, all Beasts of thickets and of rocks.*

Sing, Creatures, sing,
*   Angels and Men and Birds and everything.*

All notes of Doves
*   Fill all our world: this is the time of loves.*

How We Celebrate Easter

Cass R. Sandak

Easter is a time of joy. The Easter season celebrates the coming of spring. As a religious holiday, Easter Sunday celebrates Christ's resurrection. Christians believe that Jesus rose from the dead on Easter Sunday nearly two thousand years ago. Easter means new life—a new beginning. It is a time for all people to be happy.

In many places, cold weather keeps people inside most of the winter. In the spring, life begins again outdoors. Birds sing in the trees. Flowers bloom. Baby chicks hatch from their eggs. All these things show the wonders of spring.

In the spring the sun rises earlier and earlier each day. Days grow longer and become warmer. Because of this, long ago people of different races and religions held spring festivals.

Easter is our spring festival. No one knows for sure where the name *Easter* comes from. Some people think that it comes from the direction East, where the sun rises.

The Anglo-Saxons were people who lived in England more than a thousand years ago. They called a whole month *Eastur-monath*. This means the "month of the growing sun." It was about the same month we call April. The name *April* comes from a Latin word that means "to open." April is the month when buds swell and open. We open our doors and go out into the fresh air.

Easter is the oldest Christian holiday. It has been a church festival since the time of Jesus' earliest followers. Early churches could not agree on a date for Easter. In the year A.D. 325, however, the Council of Nicaea (ny-SEE-uh) chose the day on which we celebrate Easter.

The date of Easter changes from year to year, but it is always on a Sunday. It may come as early as March 22 or as late as April 25. Easter may be on any Sunday between these two dates.

The date of Easter depends on the moon and the sun and on the date of the vernal equinox. *Vernal* means spring. *Equinox* comes from two Latin words that mean "equal night."

The equinox is a day when there are the same number of hours of sunlight and of darkness. This happens twice each year, once in the spring and once in the autumn. The usual date for the spring equinox is March 21. But the actual time when day and night are the same length may come a day or two earlier or later.

Easter is always the Sunday following the first full moon on or after the vernal equinox.

After the vernal equinox, days get longer as the sun rises earlier and sets later. The Anglo-Saxons called the spring season *Lenctentid,* which means "the time of lengthening." We take our word *Lent* from this Old English word for spring.

Lent is the time of year that leads up to Easter. It begins on Ash Wednesday, when many Christians go to church services. Often at these services the priest or minister uses ashes to make a cross on each person's forehead. The ashes come from palm branches that have been burned.

Because the date of Easter changes, Ash Wednesday also comes on a different date each year.

Lent is a time of fasting. Fasting is a word that has two meanings. It can mean eating no food. At breakfast, we break the fast that we have kept all night. Or fasting can mean eating lightly.

Many people think fasting is good for their health. Or they may fast for religious reasons. For hundreds of years, most people did not eat meat, cheese, butter, fat, and eggs during Lent. Nowadays we often give up something we enjoy, like candy or sweets.

Fasts during Lent probably began from a need to make food supplies last longer. In earlier times, very little food from the last harvest was left by the beginning of spring. It was a good idea to give up some things during this time.

There are 46 days between Ash Wednesday and Easter. But since Sundays during this time are not fast days, the actual length of Lent is 40 days. Lent ends the day before Easter.

When Lent begins, Christians try to understand Jesus' last days on earth.

The last week of Lent is called Holy Week. In the days leading up to Easter Sunday, Christians remember the story of Christ's death and resurrection.

The Sunday before Easter is called Palm Sunday. Many churches hand out palm branches or little crosses made from palms on this day. This marks the day Jesus came into Jerusalem. His followers waved palm branches to greet him. This was a sign of respect. Jesus had come to the city to celebrate the Jewish Passover.

Passover comes at about the same time as the Christian Holy Week. Passover lasts for eight days. It is one of the most important Jewish holidays. During Passover, Jews remember how Moses led his people out of Egypt, where they were slaves, hundreds of years before the birth of Christ.

During Holy Week, services are held every day in many churches.

The Thursday of Holy Week is often called Maundy Thursday. *Maundy* comes from a Latin word that means "a command." Jesus commanded his followers to love one another.

On the first Maundy Thursday, Jesus ate with his friends for the last time. Many artists have painted this meal, which is called the "Last Supper." Later the same evening, Judas, one of Jesus' friends, had him arrested. The next day, Friday, Jesus was brought to trial, though he had done nothing wrong.

The Friday of Holy Week is called Good Friday. This name probably comes from "God's Friday." Christians believe that Jesus was God's Son.

On Good Friday, Jesus was nailed to a wooden cross. Several hours later he died. This kind of death is called a crucifixion. Long ago, many people were put to death in this way.

The cross on which Jesus died has become an important sign of the Christian faith. During Lent, some people take part in a devotion called the Stations of the Cross. The 14 "stations" are prayers and readings about Christ's trial and crucifixion.

After the crucifixion on Good Friday, Jesus' friends put his body in a tomb. The following Sunday morning, three women went to the tomb. There they found an angel who told them that Jesus was gone. He had risen from the dead. This was the first Easter Sunday.

Later, Jesus' friends saw him, spoke with him, and touched him. Then, as people watched, Jesus rose up to heaven.

Church services during Holy Week are serious and quiet. Church bells are not rung between Maundy Thursday and Easter Sunday. Children in some countries are told that the bells have gone to Rome to visit the Pope. The bells then fly back home early Easter morning, bringing the decorated eggs that are left in baskets for the children.

In early times, people placed their Easter eggs in grass nests that were made to look like birds' nests. Later, baskets filled with straw took the places of nests. Today, Easter baskets are decorated with ribbons, flowers, and straw. They are filled with eggs, jelly beans, and other Easter sweets. A chocolate rabbit or yellow marshmallow chick is a welcome sight in an Easter basket, especially if you gave up candy or sweets for Lent!

Many Easter customs come from Europe, where eggs have been decorated for hundreds of years. These eggs are said to be brought by the Easter rabbit.

The eggs used for dyeing or painting are usually hen's eggs, or other birds' eggs. But some early people celebrated the beginning of spring by dancing around a pile of snakes' eggs. The people of ancient Persia gave each other eggs dyed red on the first day of spring. The Chinese still present gifts of eggs to the parents of newborn children. Around the world, the egg, like the seed, is a sign of life.

Throughout Eastern and Central Europe, making Easter eggs is taken very seriously. The most elaborate eggs are probably those decorated by people from Poland and from the Ukraine, a part of the Soviet Union. These people call their eggs *pysanki,* which means "written eggs."

The eggs are decorated in a way that is like writing. A type of pen is used to draw signs and pictures on the eggs with wax. Then the eggs are dyed. The dye will not stay where the wax has been placed. When the dyeing is finished, the wax is melted off and leaves a design.

Other groups have their own ways of making Easter eggs. The Pennsylvania Dutch dye their eggs. Then they scratch the shells with a knife or needle. This scrapes away a little of

the dye and makes a lacy white pattern on the shell.

Probably the most beautiful Easter eggs are not real eggs at all! About one hundred years ago, a jeweler named Carl Faberge lived in Russia. He made eggs out of gold, silver, and jewels. At Easter time, the Russian Czar or Emperor gave these eggs as gifts. Almost always the eggs open up and show a surprise—perhaps tiny figures of people and animals.

Museums may have collections of all kinds of beautiful Easter eggs that are more than a hundred years old.

Today we may make Easter eggs in a simpler way. Easter tints are often used. These are robins' egg blue, the pale yellow of a newly hatched chick, the purple of violets, or the light green grass on a spring morning. You may enjoy hanging your Easter eggs on an egg tree. The Pennsylvania Dutch set up the first egg trees.

According to folklore, a German duchess started the custom of hiding brightly decorated eggs. These were said to have been left by the Easter rabbit for the country children. The children then made a game of finding the eggs.

Sometimes the Easter egg hunt is a treasure hunt. The hiding places are given in written clues. The treasure hunt is finished when all the eggs have been found. The person who puts the most eggs into his or her basket wins the game.

In the early 1800s, Dolley Madison, the wife of President James Madison, the fourth president of the United States, began the Easter Egg Roll in Washington, D.C. This event is still held each year on Easter Monday. For about the first 50 years, the egg roll took place near the Capitol Building. Since the 1860s, it has been held on the White House lawn. Children roll eggs down a hill to see which egg will go the farthest without breaking.

Because Easter marks the rebirth of nature, many of its signs are outdoor things—animals and plants.

The animals we think of most often at Easter are chickens, lambs, and rabbits. The lamb is a sign of good luck at Easter. In many places, cakes and chocolate are made in the shape of a lamb.

Because rabbits give birth to five or six litters of babies each year, they stand for the richness of nature. German settlers brought the idea of the Easter rabbit to the United States in the late 1700s.

Plants and flowers are important parts of Easter. They make nice Easter gifts. Women often wear orchids or other flowers on Easter Sunday.

Many kinds of bulb flowers bloom in the spring. Though the flowers seem delicate, they are hardy and strong. The bulbs lie in the cold ground all winter. Crocuses may bloom even while there is snow on the ground. Daffodils and tulips come later.

Perhaps more than any other flower, lilies stand for Easter. For hundreds of years, religious pictures have shown different kinds of lilies. Lily flowers are shaped liked bells or trumpets. They remind people of joyful music. Their sweet smell and simple form seem to stand for everything pure and perfect.

Many countries have traditional Easter foods. Hot cross buns have long been popular in both Great Britain and the United States. The buns are sweet rolls filled with raisins. They are marked with a cross made from sugar frosting.

At first, hot cross buns were baked and eaten only on Good Friday. But they became so popular that now they are baked all through Lent. People in other countries bake many different kinds of Easter breads and cakes.

For the Easter meal, many families have ham. Ham is smoked pork that comes from pigs. In many countries the pig is a sign of good luck and wealth. That is why small banks are often piggy banks.

In some countries, especially Italy, Greece, and parts of the Middle East, the Easter meat is roast lamb.

The Easter walk is an old custom. After Easter services in the Middle Ages, townspeople in their finery walked from church into the fields.

The Easter walk lives on in the Easter parades that are held in many cities. In New York City, thousands of people turn out to see crowds walking down Fifth Avenue. In London, the Easter Parade is held in Battersea Park.

For a long time, people have worn new clothes on Easter. In fact, some people think that it is bad luck not to wear at least one new piece of clothing. On Easter Sunday many women wear a new hat—an "Easter bonnet."

In earlier times, a young man would send a pair of gloves to his sweetheart. This was a proposal of marriage. If she accepted his offer, she wore the gloves on Easter morning.

Churches all over the world hold services on Easter morning. Bells ring and people sing joyful hymns. The word *Alleluia* is often heard. This means "Praise God." Because of Christ's resurrection, Christians are filled with hope and joy.

Easter is an important religious holiday, and it is more than that. It is a time for everyone to be glad. Decorated eggs, Easter baskets, and lilies are all signs of Easter. They show the joy of life in the coming of springtime and in the rebirth of nature.

Easter Day, Glad Easter Day

Easter Day, glad Easter Day!
Winter's snows have gone away;
Birds and flow'rs awake and sing
To the ris'n Lord and King.

Easter Day, glad Easter Day!
Christ is ris'n, the angels say;
Sing, O Christian children, sing,
To the ris'n Lord and King.

Todd's Search for Spring   Margaret Springer

*I*t was Easter Sunday afternoon. Todd had a new Sunday school paper. He put it up carefully on the door of the fridge. There was a picture of daffodils and tulips and sunshine and children going to church in their new spring clothes.

Todd looked out the window. No daffodils or tulips or sunshine out there. Just piles of dirty, slushy old snow. And the children were all in their snowsuits.

"Spring has forgotten to come," said Todd.

His dad smiled. "It sure is snowy," he said. "But spring will come soon."

"I'm tired of all this snow," said Todd. "It's too yucky to make snow people out of. It's too old and mushy to toboggan on. If spring is coming, where does it come from? And where is spring now?"

"Spring is south of here," said Mom. "Gradually the warm weather creeps northward. Somewhere to the south of us the robins are singing and the flowers are growing."

"I'd like to go there," said Todd, "and tell spring to hurry up."

"Spring comes very slowly," said Dad. "But there are clues that spring is coming. Even when there's snow everywhere."

"And when you find enough clues," said Mom, "then spring comes at last."

Todd shook his head. "There's snow everywhere," he said. "Spring has forgotten to come. But I'll go and look, just in case."

Mom helped Todd put on his snowsuit. "This snowsuit is getting too small for you, Todd," she said. "Your arms and legs are sticking out."

Todd looked down at his snowsuit. It did feel kind of tight. "Is that my first clue?" asked Todd. "Does that mean spring is coming?"

"It means you're growing fast." said Dad. "But I guess it's a sort of clue. See what other clues you can find."

Todd went outside. But he didn't find one other clue—just dirty old, cold old, snowy old snow.

"I told you," said Todd when he came back inside, "spring has forgotten to come."

That evening they went to Grandmother's for Easter dinner.

"Last time you were here," said Grandmother, "you helped me light the candles, Todd. Remember?"

"Yes," said Todd, "I remember. And it was real dark outside. Hey—that's another clue!"

"That's right," said Mom. "That's a good one. The days are longer, and it's not dark at suppertime."

They told Grandmother about looking for clues.

"Todd is smart," said Grandmother. "I know he'll find lots of clues if he looks hard."

Todd looked very hard for days and days and days. But he didn't find even one.

One day he was playing with his blocks, making a tower and a castle on the floor of the living room.

"Shut your eyes, Todd," said Mom, "and tell me if you smell something."

Todd shut his eyes and sniffed. "Nice," he said. "What is it?" He opened his eyes.

Todd's mom held out a pot with three flowers in it. "They're narcissus," she said. "Remember those bulbs we planted and put in the kitchen window? Now they're blooming."

"Another clue," said Todd. "Spring is practicing on indoor flowers, but I wish it would hurry up and come outside."

"So do I," said Mom. "Look! It's snowing!"

Todd ran to the window. Big, fat, fluffy snowflakes swirled through the air. It snowed for a while. Then the snow changed to rain.

Todd watched the raindrops chase each other down the windowpane. It rained all afternoon and all evening. It was still raining when Todd went to bed.

"Hurry up, spring!" said Todd. "We need some sunshine and flowers!" But still it rained and rained.

In the morning Todd looked out of his bedroom window. It had stopped raining. Everything looked soggy and wet.

"This is worse than yesterday," said Todd at breakfast. "Spring has forgotten to come, for sure."

"Maybe," said Mom, "But maybe not."

Todd thought for a while. "Rain is a clue, Mom. Right? Is that what you were thinking?"

His mom nodded. "And other things," she said.

"I'll go outside," said Todd, "and look for clues one more time. If I don't find any today, then I'll give up."

Todd put on his snowsuit jacket, and went outside.

"Yuck!" he said. Some of the snow had melted, but there were still big patches of dirty snow everywhere. And where the snow had gone, there was mud and old dead grass, and scraps of paper garbage left over from winter. "Yuck!" said Todd again.

Then Todd heard something he hadn't heard for a long time. It was the sound of water gurgling and splashing. The edges of the snow patches were melting into tiny rivers that flowed into the drains.

Todd stood still and listened. Birds were singing, too. They were just little sparrows, but they were singing. They sang, and they chirped, and they splashed in the puddles.

A squirrel ran across the lawn, a brown, bushy-tailed, busy squirrel. Todd stood very still. The squirrel ran to the base of a tree, and dug up some nuts from the muddy ground.

Todd went around the side of his house. It felt warmer there, out of the wind. There was no snow next to the house and the earth there was brown and dry and soft. Suddenly Todd noticed something green. He stooped down and gently pushed some old leaves out of the way. A few tiny green shoots were just peeping out of the earth.

There were still big patches of snow everywhere. There were still no flowers. The sun was not shining, and it was cold. It was still not one bit like that Sunday school paper.

But all at once, sniffing the nice earthy smell down there close to the ground, Todd knew he had found enough clues. All at once he knew that spring had not forgotten. Spring had come at last.

Adopt a Grandma

Alice Sullivan Finlay

Kelly stared at the church newsletter in front of her. "I'm not sure this will work, Mom," she said.

"What can we lose by helping with the project?"

Kelly shrugged. Her mother had a point. Still, she had doubts about it. "Adopt a grandmother for Easter," the article read. "So many senior citizens are lonely and have no family. Call us at the church office if you are interested."

So Kelly's mother had called the minister to set up an appointment with an older woman who was a member of the church.

Kelly glanced out the kitchen window. *It won't make up for losing Grandma*, she thought. Tears misted her view of the backyard. Around this time last year she had been helping

Grandma plant those tulips that were now blooming bright yellow and red. She missed her grandmother so much.

"OK, Mom. We can try it. But it won't make up for Grandma not being here."

Her mother squeezed her shoulder. "I know that, honey. But maybe we both need a grandmother right now."

After school Kelly ran home and tossed her books on her bed. She changed into a nice blouse and pair of slacks. *I hope I like this Mrs. Simmons*, she thought.

As they strode up the path to the small house, Kelly's knees felt weak.

Mrs. Simmons came to the door, a frown on her face. "Come in, come in." She waved them inside.

She doesn't act happy to see us,

thought Kelly. But what did she expect? The woman didn't know them yet.

"Iced tea?" asked Mrs. Simmons.

Kelly smacked her lips, but her mother said. "Don't go to any trouble."

"Then have a seat."

Wiggling in her chair, Kelly could hardly think of a thing to say. "Uhm. Do you like flowers?" The words seemed to stick in her throat. "I used to help my grandma with the garden."

"I used to work outside, but my arthritis is so bad now."

"I—I'm sorry," Kelly murmured.

Kelly's mother came to her rescue. "We're glad the minister started this project. You see, my mother—Kelly's grandmother—died about this time last year."

"That's too bad," said Mrs. Simmons. Again, she was silent for a long while.

Kelly wanted to run out of that house and never come back. Feeling foolish, she asked, "Do you quilt or crochet? I used to help Grandma with all her projects."

"Not much anymore," said Mrs. Simmons. She looked uncomfortable, then added, "To tell you the truth, I didn't want to do this, but the minister talked me into it. I guess I'm just not the typical grandmother type. You see, I never had children of my own."

What do I say to that? Kelly wondered. Now, more than ever, she wanted to run out. Mrs. Simmons must have said yes to the minister for some reason. If Mrs. Simmons was

proud, Kelly decided, she'd do her best to be patient.

"We want you over for Easter dinner," Kelly said. "That is, if you're not going anywhere else."

"I guess I could. . . ."

"If it's all right with you, we could pick you up for church on Easter morning," said Kelly's mother. "You could spend the day with us."

"That would be fine," said Mrs. Simmons.

Glad that they had stayed only a few more minutes, Kelly raced out the door ahead of her mother. She hadn't known how hard adopting a grandmother could be. But she liked Mrs. Simmons, gruffness and all. She'd just have to try harder on Easter Sunday.

The day came too quickly, Kelly thought, as she forked scrambled eggs into her mouth at breakfast. Her mother came into the kitchen. "That dress looks great on you, Mom," Kelly said.

"You look nice, too, honey."

When they arrived at her house, Mrs. Simmons seemed in a better mood than the last time. Kelly felt a pang of sadness when she realized this was the last day they would have to see her—unless something changed, of course. *Why do I care about her anyway?* Kelly wondered. *She doesn't seem to want to get close to Mom and me.*

Mrs. Simmons put on her hat and gloves.

"You look great," said Kelly.

"Why, both of you do, too. I like little girls dressing up."

Kelly almost blurted out, "I'm not a little girl," but she stopped herself.

When they got to church, the minister greeted them outside the front door. "I'm glad to see you, Mrs. Simmons," he said, as if he hadn't seen her for a while.

"Happy Easter, Reverend." She put her chin higher in the air and walked to the first row.

The minister nodded to Kelly. "Keep up the good work."

If I am doing any good, Kelly thought. She padded down the aisle and sat between her mother and Mrs. Simmons.

In his sermon, the minister talked about unselfish love. Kelly thought she saw tears in Mrs. Simmons' eyes. *Is Mrs. Simmons hard to get along with because she never had a family?* Kelly wondered.

Then, thinking about her own grandmother, Kelly cried too. Her mother put her arm on her shoulder. The tears eased the ball of pain that had grown in her stomach. *It should have been Grandma with us this year*, Kelly thought. Then she chased the thought away.

Please, Lord, she prayed silently, *Help me feel better. There's nothing I can do. I can't bring Grandma back. But if Mrs. Simmons needs us, help us be nice to her.*

As if Mrs. Simmons heard the prayer, she looked down at Kelly, then squeezed her hand. "Don't cry, little one," she said. "I know how it is to lose your grandmother. I lost mine a long, long time ago."

After the service, Kelly walked outside. Peace and warmth flooded through her. Smelling a daffodil, she waited for Mrs. Simmons and her mother to come out. *Maybe I can ask Mrs. Simmons to teach me how to cook*, she thought, *or go for short walks.* She knew now that their relationship would take time to grow.

When she saw them coming, Kelly grabbed Mrs. Simmons' hand. *Thank you, Lord*, she prayed. *I guess we did need a grandmother after all.*

Eggs! Eggs! Eggs!
Paula DePaolo

Sarah and Roger got up with the sun, for it was the morning of Mrs. Fleagle's Easter egg hunt. Roger had always been too little to go on one of her hunts, but this year he was four and old enough to go with Sarah.

Just before ten o'clock they excitedly walked to Mrs. Fleagle's house. It stood at the end of Maple Street like a beautiful white castle. Mrs. Fleagle's favorite friends were the children on Maple Street. They loved to play at her house. The yard was gigantic, and Mrs. Fleagle made picnic lunches for them to eat under the trees. She shared her big house with her two beagles, Pork Chop and Ham Bone, and her butler Mr. Corbett.

Mrs. Fleagle was standing on her porch waving to the children. She was wearing a lavender spring dress, and a daffodil was pinned in her white hair. A lacy handkerchief was tucked into her pocket, and around her neck hung a whistle.

"Hi! Mrs. Fleagle," called Sarah.

"Hi!" said Roger.

"Welcome to my Easter egg hunt," said Mrs. Fleagle. "It is going to be a day to remember."

Sarah sat on the porch steps. She remembered some of Mrs. Fleagle's other Easter egg hunts. They had all been days to remember because Mrs. Fleagle always forgot to do something. One year she forgot to invite the children. The next year Mrs. Fleagle remembered the children and forgot to hide the eggs. This year everyone was invited, and Sarah saw eggs scattered about the yard. So what could . . . ?

She felt a tap on her shoulder. "Oh, hi, Miranda," she said. "I was just wondering what Mrs. Fleagle forgot this year."

"I know what she didn't forget," said Miranda. She pointed toward Mrs. Fleagle's kitchen window. Sitting on a table near the window was a huge chocolate rabbit. It was the prize for the child who found the most eggs.

"Isn't it beautiful!" Sarah exclaimed.

"Look at his candy eyes," said Miranda, "and the basket of jelly beans he's holding."

"And the foil-wrapped eggs around his feet," said Sarah. "They're so yummy! Oh, I hope I win."

"I want to win too," said Roger. "I hope I find the most eggs of all."

By ten o'clock everyone had arrived—Sarah, Roger, Miranda, the twins Stacy and Tracy, Stuart, Kim, Willie, Mrs. Fleagle's 15 great-grandchildren, and mean Angel Ellerbee. Mr. Corbett, dressed in his fanciest butler uniform, put paper sacks side by side in line for each child. Mrs. Fleagle waved her lacy handkerchief and the children were off, the beagles barking with excitement.

Sarah and Roger followed a path that ran between a fence and a row of pine trees. Eggs peeked out at them from everywhere. One year Mrs. Fleagle forgot to ᴄᴏᴏ ɪᴇ eggs but this year she had remembered. Sarah saw striped ones and polᴊ dot ones, rainbow-colored ones and some with pictures of ducks and lᴀ ᴜbs. She and Roger picked eggs out of the shrubbery and from under leaves. Willie was looking under heavy rocks, and Stacy and Tracy quarreled over who saw the green and yellow speckled egg first.

"Sarah! Sarah!" called Roger. "I found the biggest, fattest worm in the whole world."

"Roger," said Sarah, "you can't win a prize for finding a fat worm. Hurry or the eggs will all be gone!"

Roger found one more egg. Then he started to put pinecones in his bag. Sarah reminded him of the chocolate rabbit.

They ran over to join Stuart and Kim at the fish pond. Eggs were hidden in the flowers all around it. While the other children picked them up, Roger counted his eggs and pinecones.

"Oh, oh," said Willie, "here comes trouble." Mean Angel Ellerbee was coming toward them. Angel had a lot of eggs in her bag already, but she wanted to make sure she had the most.

"Miranda," she threatened, "if you don't give me four of your eggs, I'll tell your mother you cut your doll's hair." Miranda gave her four eggs.

"Stuart," she said, "weren't you the one who walked in the wet cement in front of Mrs. Kelsey's house? For six eggs I'll be quiet." Stuart gave her six eggs.

Angel grabbed one of Roger's eggs from his bag. He looked as though he were going to cry, so Sarah gave him one of hers.

"You're cheating," said Sarah. "Cheaters can't win."

"Oh, yeah!?" said Angel. "Just watch."

Sarah saw her take two eggs each from Stacy and Tracy and snatch some from other small children.

At eleven o'clock Mrs. Fleagle blew her whistle. The hunt was over. Everyone met back at the house. All the children had found eggs, but Angel's bag was the fullest.

"Please bring out the prizes, Mr. Corbett," instructed Mrs. Fleagle. "Then we'll count the eggs."

"Well," Angel said. "I guess I'm the big winner." But then she spotted another egg under the porch. She grabbed it and dropped it into her bag. R-r-r-rip! The bottom started to fall out of her bag. Miranda reached out to help, but Angel pulled the bag tightly to her chest.

C-r-r-r-unch!

"They're mine, all mine!" she cried as the eggs crashed to the driveway. Then everyone saw what Mrs. Fleagle had forgotten to do this year—the eggs hadn't been cooked! Raw eggs soaked into Angel's dress and made it stick to her skin. They dripped down her legs and into her shoes. Her hands were covered with sticky yolks, and gooey whites ran down her arms. Pork Chop and Ham Bone hurried over and happily lapped up the eggs.

"I'm the winner," Angel yelled. But no one could tell now how many eggs Angel had really collected.

The grand prize went to Percival, one of Mrs. Fleagle's great-grandchildren. He had found 22 eggs. Sarah won a chocolate chick, and Roger a big bag of jelly beans.

"Thank you, Mrs. Fleagle," called the children as they started for home.

"This really was a day to remember," Sarah said to Roger. And, munching his jelly beans, he nodded his head in complete agreement!

Easter Song

Mary A. Lathbury

Snowdrops, lift your timid heads,
All the earth is waking,
Field and forest, brown and dead,
Into life are waking;
Snowdrops, rise and tell the story
How he rose, the Lord of glory.

Lilies! Lilies! Easter calls,
Rise to meet the dawning
Of the blessed light that falls
Thro' the Easter morning;
Ring your bells and tell the story,
How he rose, the Lord of glory.

Waken, sleeping butterflies,
Burst your narrow prison;
Spread your golden wings and rise,

For the Lord is risen;
Spread your wings and tell the story,
How he rose, the Lord of glory.

The Selfish Giant
Oscar Wilde

Every afternoon, as they were coming from school, the children would go to the Giant's garden.

It was a large, lovely garden, with soft green grass. Here and there over the grass stood beautiful flowers like stars, and there were 12 peach trees that in the springtime broke out into delicate blossoms of pink and pearl, and in the autumn bore rich fruit.

The birds sat in the trees and sang so sweetly that the children used to stop their games to listen to them. "How happy we are here!" they cried to each other.

One day the Giant came back. He had been to visit a friend, the Cornish Ogre, and had stayed with him for seven years. After the seven years were over he had said all that he had to say, for his conversation was limited, and he determined to return to his own castle. When he arrived he saw the children playing in the garden.

"What are you doing here?" he cried in a very gruff voice, and the children ran away.

"My own garden is my own garden," said the Giant. "Anyone can understand that, and I will allow nobody to play in it but myself." So he built a high wall all around it, and put up a notice board: *Trespassers will be prosecuted.*

He was a very selfish giant.

The poor children had nowhere to play. They tried to play on the road, but the road was dusty and full of hard stones, and they did not like it. They used to wander round the high wall, when their lessons were over, and talk about the beautiful garden inside. "How happy we were there," they said to each other.

Then the Spring came, and all over the country there were little blossoms and little birds. But in the garden of the Selfish Giant it was still Winter. The birds did not care to sing in it, as there were no children, and the trees forgot to blossom.

Once a beautiful flower put its head out from the snow but when it saw the notice board it was so sorry for the children that it slipped back into the ground again, and went off to sleep. The only people who were pleased were the Snow and the Frost. "Spring has forgotten this garden," they cried, "so we will live here all the year round."

The Snow covered up the grass with her great white cloak, and the Frost painted all the trees silver. Then they invited the North Wind to stay with them, and he came. He was wrapped in furs, and he roared all day about the garden and blew the chimney-pots down. "This is a delightful spot," he said. "We must ask the Hail to visit."

So Hail came. Every day for three hours he rattled the roof of the castle till he broke most of the slates, and then he ran round and round the garden as fast as he could go. He was dressed in grey, and his breath was like ice.

"I cannot understand why the Spring is so late in coming," said the selfish Giant, as he sat at the window and looked at his cold, white garden. "I hope the weather will change."

But the Spring never came, nor the Summer. The Autumn gave golden fruit to every garden, but to the Giant's garden she gave none. "He is too selfish," she said. So it was always Winter there, and the North Wind, and the Hail, and the Frost, and the Snow danced about through the trees.

One morning the Giant was lying awake in bed when he heard some lovely music. It sounded so sweet to his ears that he thought it must be the King's musicians passing by. It was only a little linnet singing outside his window, but it was so long since he had heard a bird sing in his garden that it seemed to him to be the most beautiful music in the world.

Then the Hail stopped dancing over his head, and the North Wind ceased roaring, and a delicious perfume came to him through the open casement. "I believe the Spring has come at last," said the Giant, and he jumped out of bed and looked out.

What did he see?

He saw the most beautiful sight. Through a little hole in the wall the children had crept in, and they were sitting in the branches of the trees. In every tree

that he could see, there was a little child. And the trees were so glad to have the children back again that they had covered themselves with blossoms and were waving their arms gently above the children's heads. The birds were flying about and twittering with delight, and the flowers were looking up through the green grass and laughing.

It was a lovely scene; only in one corner was it still Winter. It was the farthest corner of the garden, and in it was standing a little boy. He was so small that he could not reach up to the branches of the tree, and he was wandering about it, crying bitterly. The poor tree was still quite covered with frost and snow, and the North Wind was blowing and roaring above it. "Climb up, little boy!" said the tree, and it bent its branches down as low as it could; but the boy was too tiny.

And the Giant's heart melted as he looked out. "How selfish I have been!" he said. "Now I know why the Spring would not come here. I will put that poor little boy on the top of the tree, and then I will knock down the wall, and my garden shall be the children's playground for ever and ever."

So he crept downstairs and opened the front door quite softly and went out into the garden. But when the children saw him they were so frightened that they all ran away, and Winter came to the garden again. Only the little boy did not run, for his eyes were so full of tears that he did not see the Giant coming. And the Giant strode up behind him and took him gently in his hand, and put him up into the tree.

The tree broke at once into blossom, and the birds came and sang in it, and the little boy stretched out his two arms and flung them around the Giant's neck, and kissed him. And the other children, when they saw the Giant was not wicked any longer, came running back; and with them came the Spring.

"It is your garden now, little children," said the Giant, and he took a great axe and knocked down the wall. And when the people were going to market at twelve o'clock they found the Giant playing with the children in the most beautiful garden they had ever seen.

All day long they played, and in the evening they came to the Giant to bid him good-bye.

"But where is your little companion?" he said. "The boy I put in the tree." The giant loved him best because he had kissed him.

"We don't know," answered the children. "He has gone away."

"You must tell him to be sure and come tomorrow," said the Giant. But the children said that they did not know where he lived and had never seen him before, and the Giant felt very sad.

Every afternoon when school was over, the children came and played with the Giant. But the little boy whom the Giant loved was never seen again. The Giant was very kind to all the children, yet he longed for his first little friend and often spoke of him. "How I would like to see him," he would say.

Years went by, and the Giant grew old and feeble. He could not play about any more, so he sat in a huge armchair, and watched the children at their games, and admired his garden. "I have many beautiful flowers," he said, "but the children are the most beautiful flowers of all."

One winter morning he looked out of his window as he was dressing. He did not hate the Winter now, for he knew that it was merely Spring asleep, and that the flowers were resting.

Suddenly he rubbed his eyes in wonder, and looked and looked. It certainly was a marvelous sight. In the farthest corner of the garden was a tree quite covered with lovely white blossoms. Its branches were all golden, and silver fruit hung down from them, and underneath stood the little boy he had loved.

Downstairs ran the Giant, in great joy, and out into the garden. He hastened across and came near to the child. And when he came quite close his face grew red with anger, and he said, "Who hath dared to wound thee?" For on the palms of the child's hands were the prints of two nails, and the prints of two nails on the little feet.

"Who hath dared to wound thee?" cried the Giant. "Tell me, that I may take my big sword and slay him."

"Nay!" answered the child. "But these are the wounds of Love."

"Who are you?" asked the Giant, and a strange awe fell on him, and he knelt before the Little Child.

And the child smiled on the Giant and said to him, "You let me play once in your garden; today you shall come with me to my garden, which is Paradise."

And when the children ran in that afternoon, they found the Giant lying dead under the tree, all covered with white blossoms.

Snowbound at Easter

Florence Wightman Rowland

Jerryann pressed her nose against the shiny pane of the train window. Her blue eyes anxiously watched the snowflakes as they fell steadily.

Any little girl of six would have been glad to welcome a snowstorm if it had been Christmas time. But this wasn't Christmas. It was the day before Easter.

Jerryann's grandmother lived up in the high hills, and often the little girl had gone on this very train to see her—but not like this. Always before Mother-Ann or Daddy-Jerry had been with her. This time she was alone, and that was quite different. Of course she wasn't really entirely alone, for Uncle John was the conductor on this mountain train; and he would keep his eye on her and see that she got off at Grandmother's station. But Uncle John wasn't the same as Mother or Daddy.

Mother-Ann had packed a nice lunch in a brown paper bag for Jerryann; and Daddy-Jerry had driven them to the station. Jerryann had bravely waved good-bye as she had clung to Uncle John's big, rough hand.

But now Jerryann was going farther and farther away from home every minute—and somehow it seemed very much farther with the clouds so gray and heavy with snow!

Jerryann tried hard to swallow a funny lump that kept coming up in her throat.

Just then Uncle John came through the train to take up the tickets.

"Well, well," he said to Jerryann, "it looks as if the Easter Bunny won't be able to make it this year through all this snow!"

Uncle John was only teasing. Not being used to little girls just six who were in the habit of expecting the Easter Bunny, he didn't realize how important the Easter Bunny was to Jerryann.

Jerryann nodded her head. But when Uncle John had gone by, she just couldn't swallow the funny lump any longer, and the next moment two great tears rolled down her cheeks. She took out the clean handkerchief that Mother-Ann had put in her pocket at the last minute and wiped her eyes.

"Ahemmm! Ahemmm! Ahemmm!"

Jerryann looked around at the man, and her tear-filled blue eyes met a pair of very kind brown ones. Then the man smiled, and Jerryann smiled back through her tears.

"Did I hear somebody say something about the Easter Bunny not being able to get through the snow?" the man said.

"I guess you did," answered Jerryann politely. "That was Uncle John."

"Oh," said the man. "Of course Uncle John knows a lot about a lot of things. But I'm sure he doesn't know anything about Easter Bunnies. I've been told that they love snowstorms!"

Jerryann and the man both began to laugh, and after that they became very good friends.

His name was Mr. Ferris, he told her, and he was an artist. He had a little cabin in the mountains not far from Grandmother's home. Here he often went to paint the beautiful trees and birds and flowers and sunsets.

It made Jerryann feel very much at home to know that Mr. Ferris lived not far from Grandmother and that once he had bought some eggs from her. So pretty soon Jerryann didn't feel lonely any more at all.

By and by it became dark; and as it was getting near Jerryann's bedtime, she began to grow sleepy. Mr. Ferris suggested that she eat her lunch while he went into the other car to look around for the Easter Bunny.

When he came back, Jerryann was curled up on her seat, fast asleep.

Pretty soon Uncle John brought his big overcoat and covered the little girl. As he was tucking her in, the train rolled slower and slower up the steep grade. Then it came to a stop!

"What is the trouble?" Mr. Ferris asked Uncle John.

"A snowslide, sir, just ahead of the engine," Uncle John answered. "It happens often up here in the mountains."

"Are we liable to be tied up long?" Mr. Ferris asked.

"I'm afraid so, sir. If the slide is very deep, we might be here eight or ten hours. We have to wait for the snowplow to come through. Sorry, sir! I hope you won't mind."

"It really doesn't matter to me," Mr. Ferris said. "I'm going up to my cabin for a rest, anyway. But that little niece of yours is going to be very much disappointed if she wakes up and finds that the Easter Bunny hasn't been around."

"I wish I knew what to do about it, sir!" said Uncle John, looking really quite disturbed.

Mr. Ferris smiled.

"I'm a first-class helper of Easter Bunnies," he said. "If I only had some hard-cooked eggs, I could turn out something that even an Easter Bunny would be proud of."

By this time the engineer and fireman had come into the train and had heard the conversation between Mr. Ferris and Uncle John.

"I have some hard-boiled eggs in my lunch box," said the engineer. "I'll get them."

"Fine!" said Mr. Ferris.

In a minute the engineer returned with three big, white, hard-cooked eggs which he handed to Mr. Ferris.

And as he and the other men hadn't anything to do, they sat about and watched the artist.

First he opened one of his flat black cases in which were tubes of many different colored paints. Then from another bag he took out scissors, some white paper, and a jar of paste. And then he sat about performing his wonders on the engineer's eggs!

Early next morning as Uncle John's train was puffing up the steep grade again, Jerryann opened her eyes. The first thing she saw were three little eggs perched upon her window sill. Jerryann sat up and rubbed her eyes hard.

"Oh, he came! He came! The Easter Bunny came!" she cried breathlessly.

Then she looked again at her Easter eggs. First there was a fat Humpty Dumpty. Next in line came a perky little rooster, so real one might have expected him to walk along the window sill. The last egg was a yellow duck. He sat looking at Jerryann as if to say, "Quack! Quack! Here I am!"

The delighted little girl laughed aloud. Then she looked across the aisle at Mr. Ferris.

"The Easter Bunny did come through the snow after all!" she said.

"Why, so he did!" agreed Mr. Ferris.

And then they both laughed and laughed and laughed.

And when Uncle John came into the car a few minutes later to tell Jerryann that they were just pulling into Grandmother's station, he found the happiest little girl in the world waiting for him.

Ivan's Easter Service Amelia W. Swayne

Ivan was a little Russian boy, who lived in the city of St. Petersburg. It was the day before Easter, and he was very happy, because he was to be allowed to go to the great church for the midnight service. His sister, Sonia, who was older than he was, had gone the year before and remembered much of what had happened.

As they set out from their home, Ivan asked, "Why is the church so dark when we go in?"

"Because people are remembering the time when everyone thought Jesus was dead," said his mother.

"That was a very dark time," said his father. "People thought the light of the world had gone out. The darkness of the church is to remind us of that time."

Soon they came to the church. As they went in, each one was given a candle. Ivan carried his very carefully, and sat down quietly beside his father. He could hear the soft music, but he could not see the great organ. Up on the altar a low light burned. The priest was beginning the service. He sang many parts of it, and the choir replied from time to time. Ivan could not understand all they were saying, but the music was very beautiful and he was glad to be sitting there, close to his father.

The priest finished his prayer, and with the other priests and the choir walked down the aisle. Ivan could hear the swish of their robes as they passed him. They left the church, and now all was very, very quiet, and very, very dark. Ivan sat as still as he could, and tried to think how the world would be if no one remembered the things that Jesus had taught.

Suddenly the great bells rang out, and the whole church seemed to become full of light. Easter Day had come! The priests and choir marched in singing joyfully, "He is risen," and everyone seemed very happy. A priest held out a shining taper, and Ivan reached up to light his candle. He now saw that the church was crowded with people all lighting candles. Soon after they had done this, the service ended, and everyone started home, carrying their lights carefully.

"Christ is risen!" said Ivan's father.

"He is risen indeed!" replied his mother.

"Christ is risen!" said Sonia.

"He is risen indeed!" said Ivan.

Ivan was very happy. He was glad that he had gone to the church. He was glad that he could carry home his bright candle.

"It would still be dark, if we were not carrying our lights, wouldn't it?" he said.

The Lamb

William Blake

Little lamb, who made thee?
Dost thou know who made thee,
Gave thee life, and bade thee feed
By the streams and o'er the mead;
Gave thee clothing of delight,
Softest clothing, woolly, bright;
Gave thee such a tender voice,
Making all the vales rejoice:
Little lamb, who made thee?
Dost thou know who made thee?

Little lamb, I'll tell thee,
Little lamb, I'll tell thee;
He is called by thy name,
For He calls Himself a Lamb;
He is meek, and He is mild,
He became a little child.
I a child, and thou a lamb,
We are called by His name.
Little lamb, God bless thee,
Little lamb, God bless thee.

The Easter Egg Tree

Joyce Nelms

Betsy did everything to keep the tears from coming. She gazed at the pink ruffled curtains and the small maple tree outside her window. Then her hand reached for the book which lay open on the bed.

But, in spite of everything, tears began to trickle slowly down her cheeks. It wasn't having to stay in bed that made Betsy cry. The doctor said she would be completely well in a few more weeks.

Tomorrow was Easter Sunday, and she would miss Sunday school and church. But that was not the cause of her tears either, because Betsy was going to watch sunrise services on television.

Betsy swallowed hard and tried not to think about the thing that was making her cry, but it wouldn't go away. The problem was her friends—her very best friends in Sunday school had completely forgotten her! This morning the mailman hadn't brought a single card or letter from anyone in her class.

Each time the telephone rang, Betsy thought it might be Debbie or Paul or one of the others from Sunday school. But the call was always for Mom or Dad or her big brother, Kevin. It was hard to believe—Betsy sighed—but the class just didn't care if she had a happy Easter!

Mother came in to get her lunch tray, and Betsy quickly dried her tears.

"You didn't finish all of your sandwich," said Mother, frowning. "I thought cream cheese and strawberry jam was your favorite."

"I'm not very hungry today," said Betsy, trying to smile.

"All right," said Mother, "I'll close the blinds now, and you try to take a nap."

When it was dark in the room, Betsy closed her eyes and tried to squeeze back the tears. Maybe if she took a nap, she could forget about being sad.

Later, when Betsy awoke, she sat up in bed wondering if she had been dreaming. There had been strange noises. She sat quietly, listening.

No, she had not been dreaming. The strange noises were coming from outside her window. There was the muffled sound of whispering voices and footsteps on the soft, new grass.

What was going on outside her window? Betsy wished she could reach the cord that would raise the blind. Now she could hear a small giggle, and just when she thought she couldn't stand the suspense any longer, Mother appeared at the door.

Betsy cried. "Please open the blind! Something is happening outside my window, and I want to see what's going on."

Mother smiled and opened the blind. Instantly, Betsy's face was as bright as the sunshine pouring into the room. "Oh!" exclaimed Betsy. "It

looks like a picture from one of my books."

The little maple tree was no longer wearing just early spring buds. It had been made into a beautiful Easter egg tree. Dozens of eggshells had been painted with colorful designs and fastened to the branches with ribbons.

Then Betsy saw Debbie and Paul and Mrs. Alexander—and her entire Sunday school class—waving to her. Moments later, Mother was inviting them all inside to have punch and cookies.

Late that afternoon, Betsy lay back on her pillows and gazed out the window at the Easter egg tree.

"What a wonderful surprise!" she thought. "I should have known my friends wouldn't forget me. And I'll never forget this Easter."

Neighbors from Cucumbers

Marcella Fisher Anderson

Mom and I had just finished our supper one evening when a pickup truck came clanging down our road. From the kitchen window we watched a family unloading their truck in the driveway and moving into the house that had been vacant for three years.

"Who are they?" I asked.

"Migrant workers, I hear," said Mom.

"Migrant workers?" I asked. "What's that?"

"Folks who move around from crop to crop and hire out to pick the harvest. Mostly they live in camps, but these folks seem to have scraped up enough money to buy the old house." Mom's thin lips tightened. "I wish them luck moving into this town. People aren't very friendly, especially to newcomers."

After I finished washing the dishes, I walked out the back door. A boy my age stood by the truck.

"Hello," I said. "Where you from?"

"Cucumbers," he replied, scarcely looking up. "And before that, peas. But we're not movin' on to potatoes this year. Papa says not. He's got himself a steady job in the sawmill."

"My name's Will," I said. "What is yours?"

"Juan."

"What grade are you in school?"

"First," he said.

"First! Why, you're as big as I am."

"I know, but I never had a chance to go to real school before."

That did it. I wasn't going to pal around with a boy my size, only in first grade. "See you later," I said.

Usually, Mom set right in making a loaf of her good bread for new neighbors, but I noticed she didn't start that night, nor any night. I didn't see anyone else go calling, either.

So I stayed away from the house and spent the time on my bike, puttering around the back roads and fishing when I could. The biggest trout I ever saw kept escaping me that summer. But the truth was, I was lonesome. And I felt cheated, too, that the first boy my age to move near was so different. With Mom working and us living outside of town, the days were long. Though I pretended the house next door wasn't there, I couldn't help but notice the family working hard in their garden.

It was the best garden I ever saw. They made neat rows by tying string between opposite stakes when they seeded. And when the peas ripened, they stripped those vines so fast I couldn't see their hands move.

One night I was in bed, nearly asleep, when I heard strange sounds in the yard next door. I climbed out of bed. Carefully, I tried to raise the window shade, but of course it snapped up. And by the time I looked out, everything was still. So I gave up and went back to bed. I must have slept because the next thing I heard was feet running hard over the dirt driveway away from the house.

The next morning the sun came in early on account of my snapped-up window shade, and I saw everything real clear. First off, I noticed the corn had been broken in half and carrots pulled up and thrown about and squash vines torn into pieces. It wasn't woodchucks but another kind of animal that did this—and there was a pair of grown-up shoeprints in the dirt to prove it.

Mom sat me down for a breakfast I couldn't eat. Halfway through my juice I heard the pickup truck next door start up and drive away. "They didn't want to go on," I said, "to potatoes or beets or anything."

"What kind of talk is that?" Mom asked. "Is that the only way those folks can talk about moving from place to place?" Then she started to cry.

"Who did it?" I demanded.

"Maybe we all did it," I said loudly. "Not one of us was friendly to them. We should at least have tried. We were their closest neighbors."

Mom wiped her eyes on a dish towel.

I left my egg half-eaten and walked outside. I didn't know what to do, so I just stared at the garden. Pretty soon I went to the shed and got out a rake.

Mom phoned the two policemen in town who came out and wrote things down. Word got around pretty fast after that.

Folks we hadn't seen for a long time came over and just raked alongside me, and some brought seedlings from their own gardens to plant. Where there was a chance for a second crop, we reseeded. Nobody laughed or told jokes.

After awhile the garden began to look pretty good again. I stood up to stretch and saw the sun warm and mellow in the sky.

We heard the muffler on the pickup truck before we saw it coming down the road and turning into the driveway. Juan's father climbed out of the cab, but he kept his hand on the door handle. He looked at the garden and at all of us. Then he stared at his feet. He didn't say anything—just opened the truck door—and the rest of the family climbed out and walked slowly into the house. He looked at me then, and I thought I saw a flicker of a smile on his face.

Everyone else started drifting away. It seemed suddenly chilly with them going. A slight breeze moved the new plants in the garden.

Suddenly, I didn't think I could stand it anymore—not joining up with a kid my own age right next door. I didn't say anything to Mom. I just walked over to the house. When I knocked on the door, Juan came right out, so he must have watched me coming.

"I have this bike," I said, as though he'd never seen me ride it. "Do you have a bike?"

His lips parted in a small smile. "I have one—not very good. I brought it from cucumbers."

"You don't mean from cucumbers," I said. "You mean from the place where you picked cucumbers. You've got to learn to talk like the rest of us if you're ever going to catch up in school."

He nodded, and a bright light came into his eyes.

"Let's go riding right after supper," I said. I thought his smile would never stop. "And tomorrow," I went on, "I'll take you to a pond where there's the biggest trout you ever saw."

After that, things seemed better. We had lots of sunny days to go fishing early in the morning. And do you know something? We finally caught that big trout—together.

Mr. Easter Rabbit

Carolyn Sherwin Bailey

A long time ago, in a far-off country, there was a famine; and this is how it came about: In the early spring, when the first grass peeped out, the sun shone so hot that the grass was dried up. No rains fell through the long summer months, so that the seed and grain that were planted could not grow, and everywhere the fields and meadows—usually so green and rich—were a dull gray-brown.

Here and there a green tree waved its dusty branches in the hot wind. When fall came, instead of the well-filled granaries and barns, there was great emptiness; and instead of happy fathers and mothers, there were grave, troubled ones.

But the children were just as happy as ever. They were glad, even, that it had not rained, for they could play out of doors all day long; and the dust-piles had never been so large and fine.

The people had to be very saving of the things that had been left from the year before. All the following winter, by being very careful, they managed to provide simple food for their families. When Christmas came there were not many presents, but the children did not miss them as we would, because in that land they did not give many presents at Christmastime.

Their holiday was Easter Sunday. On that day they had a great celebration, and there were always goodies and presents for the little boys and girls. As the time came nearer, the parents wondered what they should do for the children's holiday. Every new day it was harder than the day before to get just plain, coarse bread to eat; and where would they find all the sweetmeats and pretty things that the children had always had at Easter-time?

One evening some of the mothers met, after the children were in bed, to talk about what they should do. One mother said, "We can have eggs. All the chickens are laying; but the children are so tired of eggs, for they have them every day."

So they decided that eggs would never do for an Easter treat; and they went home sorrowfully, thinking that Easter must come and go like any other day. And one mother was more sorry than any of the others. Her dear little boy and girl had been planning and talking about the beautiful time they were to have on the great holiday.

After the mother had gone to bed, she wondered and thought if there were any way by which she could give her little ones their happy time. All at once she cried right out in the dark, "I know! I have thought of something to make the children happy!"

She could hardly wait until morning, and the first thing she did was to run into the next house and tell her neighbor of the plan she had thought of. And the neighbor told someone else, and so the secret flew until, before night, all the mothers had heard it, but not a single child.

There was still a week before Easter, so there was a good deal of whispering; and the fathers and mothers smiled every time they thought of the secret. When Easter Sunday came, everyone went, first of all, to the great stone church—mothers and fathers and children. When church was over, instead of going home, the older people suggested walking to the great woods just back of the church.

"Perhaps we may find some flowers," they said.

So on they went, and soon the merry children were scattered through the woods, among the trees.

Then a shout went up—now here, now there—from all sides.

"Father, mother, look here!"

"See what I have found—some beautiful eggs!"

"Here's a red one!"

"I've found a yellow one!"

"Here's a whole nestful—all different colors!"

And the children came running, bringing beautiful colored eggs which they had found in the soft moss under the trees. What kind of eggs could they be? They were too large for bird's eggs. They were large, like hen's eggs. But who ever saw a hen's egg so wonderfully colored?

Just then, from behind a large tree where the children had found a nest full of eggs, there jumped a rabbit, and with long leaps he disappeared in the deep woods, where he was hidden from view by the trees and bushes.

"It must be that the rabbit laid the pretty eggs," said one little girl.

"I am sure it was the rabbit," said her mother.

"Hurrah for the rabbit! Hurrah for the Easter rabbit! Hurrah for Mr. Easter Rabbit!" the children cried; and the fathers and mothers were glad with the children.

So this is the story of the first Easter eggs, for, ever since then, in that faraway land and in other countries, too, has Mr. Easter Rabbit brought the children at Eastertime some beautifully colored eggs.

At Easter Time

Laura Elizabeth Richards

The little flowers came through the ground,
  At Easter time, at Easter time;
They raised their heads and looked around,
  At happy Easter time.
And every pretty bud did say,
  "Good people, bless this holy day,
For Christ is risen, the angels say
  At happy Easter time!"

The pure white lily raised its cup
  At Easter time, at Easter time;
The crocus to the sky looked up
  At happy Easter time.
"We'll hear the song of Heaven!" they say,
  "Its glory shines on us today.
Oh! may it shine on us always
  At holy Easter time!"

'Twas long and long and long ago,
  That Easter time, that Easter time;
But still the pure white lilies blow
  At happy Easter time.
And still each little flower doth say,
  "Good Christians, bless this holy day,
For Christ is risen, the angels say
  At blessed Easter time!"

The Ugly Pink Jumper and the Beautiful Blue Dress

Margaret D. Woolington

Before Karen opened her eyes, she felt the sun on her cheeks. It was so warm she could almost imagine it was summer, but when she opened her eyes she saw the dark, bare limbs of the elm tree outside her window. It was still winter. She sighed and wiggled deeper under the blankets.

"Karen," her mother called. "Time for breakfast. We have a lot to do today."

"I know," she mumbled from beneath the covers. Saturday used to be her favorite day because she and her mom went shopping together and there was always a special treat—candy or a big double-dip chocolate cone from the ice cream shop.

Sometimes they would go to the mall. Karen especially liked it when they came home with their arms loaded with packages, and she and her mom would show their bargains to her dad.

But since her dad's accident everything had changed. Karen's dad had been in the hospital for weeks, and her mom had gone to work in an office downtown. Saturday was now a day for rushing around to the grocery store, the cleaners, the drug store. There was no time and no money for treats or shopping at the mall. Instead, they hurried through the morning and then made the hour-long drive to the hospital to see her father. The best part of Saturday was seeing her dad smile when they came into his room. How she missed him! She prayed every morning and evening that he would be home soon.

"Karen," her mother shouted. "Breakfast is ready and we have to get going."

Karen jumped up from under the warm blankets, shivering as she danced around on the cold floor, pulling on her clothes. Then she ran for the warm kitchen where she could smell the cinnamon toast and hot chocolate milk. It was her favorite Saturday food. She was thankful that hadn't changed.

During the week, after school, Karen went to Mrs. Hooper's apartment and waited for her mother to come home from work. She usually watched television or read library books, but sometimes she sat on a stool by Mrs. Hooper's sewing machine, watching her stitch pieces of material together like a jigsaw puzzle into beautiful dresses for her granddaughter, Pippa. Karen thought Pippa was the luckiest girl in the world to have a grandmother like Mrs. Hooper.

One day when Mrs. Hooper answered the door, she had in her hand a pair of scissors and a pattern, and over her arm was the most beautiful cloth Karen had ever seen. It was a soft, silky blue like a clear summer sky.

"Come into the dining room, child." Mrs. Hooper motioned her through the door. "I am going to cut out an Easter dress for my Pippa. Do you want to watch?" Karen nodded. She walked close to Mrs. Hooper so she could feel, very lightly, that lovely shimmering cloth. It was like touching a raindrop.

For two days Mrs. Hooper cut, pinned, and stitched on the material. She even gave some of the scraps to Karen to take home. Karen showed them to her mom and told her about the dress. Her mom ran her fingers over the silky material, back and forth, but she said nothing.

For the next week Karen watched the dress take shape under Mrs. Hooper's quick, darting fingers. When it was finished, she embroidered a rose bud in each corner of the large white collar and one on the white cuffs around the puffed sleeves. Then she hung it from the light fixture to "straighten out." When Karen passed by on the way to the kitchen, she would run her fingers along the silky hem.

That evening when Karen's mom came to pick her up, Karen pulled her into the dining room to see the dress. Karen's mom looked sad, although she told Mrs. Hooper that it was a lovely dress.

Karen trailed behind her mom as they walked down the hall to their apartment.

"Karen, I can't afford to buy you a new dress for Easter," her mom said.

"You don't have to buy me a dress. Mrs. Hooper could make one," Karen said. But her mother was already in the kitchen putting away the groceries, and nothing more was said about Easter or a new dress.

By the following week, the blue dress had been given to Mrs. Hooper's granddaughter. The leftover material was folded and put into a dresser drawer, and Mrs. Hooper and Karen watched cartoons on television in the afternoons.

One Saturday morning, Karen's mom called her into the bedroom. All of Karen's four dresses and her pink corduroy jumper and two blouses were lying on the bed. Her mother picked up the dresses and held them up to Karen's shoulders, measuring the fit from arm to arm and the length down the side. Finally she picked up three dresses and a blouse, leaving one dress, the pink jumper, and a cotton blouse on the bed.

"I thought you had grown a lot lately. These are way too small on you," she said. "There is a new family in church who recently lost everything in a fire. I think the girls could wear these." Then she picked up the pink jumper. "I will even have to let this hem out, you are growing so." She laid the jumper across the bed. "You can wear this for Easter."

Karen felt her eyes filling with tears. How could she tell her mom that just thinking about that beautiful blue dress made her hate her old, pink corduroy jumper.

During the long ride to the hospital that afternoon Karen was unusually quiet, thinking about what her mom had said about Easter being in your heart, not in your clothes. Why couldn't she stop wanting a beautiful blue dress like Pippa's?

Karen woke early the next morning and jumped out of bed. An idea had come to her last night when she couldn't sleep. She had suddenly remembered that leftover blue cloth that Mrs. Hooper had put away in the drawer. Maybe Mrs. Hooper would make her a dress from that. It wasn't being used for anything, and Mrs. Hooper had told Karen many times how much she enjoyed sewing. It was the perfect plan.

On Monday Karen ran from the school bus to Mrs. Hooper's apartment.

"My, you look happy today," Mrs. Hooper said to Karen when she opened the door. "What has happened to make such a big smile on your face?" She took Karen's coat. "I just baked cookies. Come into the kitchen and tell me about it."

In the kitchen Karen told Mrs. Hooper about her idea. At first Mrs. Hooper looked at Karen, then she reached over and patted her hand. "Did you ask your mother?"

"No, it's going to be a surprise."

"I see," Mrs. Hooper said and she stared at Karen for a long time without speaking. At last she stood up and walked slowly into the bedroom where she drew out the beautiful blue cloth. She came back to the kitchen and told Karen to stand by the table. First she measured the material and then she measured Karen from shoulder to shoulder and then down to her knees and around her waist. Karen was so excited she could hardly stand still.

"Ummmm," Mrs. Hooper murmured as she measured. She measured Karen, and then she measured the material again. At last she straightened up.

"Karen, I'm sorry, there just isn't enough here to make you a dress, but I might be able to make a nice underslip."

An underslip! That beautiful cloth hidden under a pink corduroy jumper? Karen jumped up and ran from the room and threw herself on the couch, burying her face in the small velveteen pillows. She heard Mrs. Hooper come over and sit beside her, waiting until Karen was able to stop crying.

After a long time, Karen sat up and dried her tears on a tissue. "It's not fair!" she said. "Nothing is fair."

"That is true." Mrs. Hooper sighed deeply. "Sometimes in this life things seem very unfair, but other times good things happen to us when we don't expect it. Life isn't all bad."

Karen turned her face toward the back of the couch. All she could think of was how her life had changed lately—her dad's accident, how he wouldn't be with them in church on Easter, her mother going to work, nothing pretty and new for Easter. It was the worst time of her life.

That evening Karen's mom seemed happier than she had been for a long time. "Did Mrs. Hooper tell you that she and her granddaughter are going to church with us on Easter? Her granddaughter just moved here. She is your age and very anxious to meet you."

Karen moaned softly, "Mom, do we have to go to church on Easter? Can't we go to the hospital instead?"

Karen's mom turned from the stove and bent down to take Karen in her arms. "I can't imagine not being in church on Easter Sunday, and that is where your father would want us to be."

Karen knew that, but the picture in her mind of sitting in her ugly pink corduroy jumper beside Pippa in her beautiful, blue silk dress was so big that she couldn't think of anything else. She would be glad when Easter was over.

On Easter Sunday morning Karen's mom came in early and opened the window. Karen felt the soft, warm breeze on her face, and she could hear a bird singing. She got out of bed and went to the window. There was a robin in the bare branches of the elm tree, and the sky was a clear blue.

"Spring is in the air," her mom said. "Better hurry and dress. We have to leave early to pick up Mrs. Hooper and Pippa."

Suddenly Karen felt sick. "Mom, I don't feel well."

Karen's mom laid her hand on Karen's forehead and looked down her throat. "You will be fine once we get to church. Oh, by the way, I got you this small bunch of flowers to pin on your pink jumper and some barrettes for your hair. When you get dressed, I'll fix them for you." She reached over and touched Karen on the cheek. "I love you," she said. "Please remember what I told you about Easter."

At Mrs. Hooper's apartment Karen hesitated in the doorway. She touched the flowers pinned to her pink jumper and remembered what her mother had said about Easter being in your heart, but Karen didn't know how to get it there.

"Karen, where are you?" her mother called. "Come in here and meet Pippa."

Karen moved silently across the entrance and into the living room.

"Pippa, this is the Karen I've told you about," Mrs. Hooper said. "Karen, this is my granddaughter, Pippa McPherson."

Pippa had long blond hair that lay like silk against the beautiful blue dress. She stood in the middle of the room holding out her hand, waiting. Karen could only stand like a statue, unable to move or speak.

Finally Pippa laughed, "Don't be afraid of the dark glasses. I am pretending to be a movie star."

Mrs. Hooper came over and guided Karen to Pippa's waiting hand. "My Pippa can't see you, but if you speak she will know where you are."

"Hello," was all Karen could manage. She was thankful when her mom said they should leave for church. In the car the two girls sat together in the back seat in silence while Karen's mom talked with Mrs. Hooper. Karen closed her eyes and tried to imagine what it was like for Pippa not to be able to see her beautiful dress, or the bare trees, or the flowers that would fill the church.

During the service the girls sat side by side. Karen watched Pippa. She knew most of the hymns by heart, and she had a beautiful voice. She sat through the long sermon, smiling and listening to each word. When she was introduced to everyone after church, Karen could see that people liked Pippa right away, and she liked them.

Later when they were getting into the car, Karen's mom said, "That is a lovely dress your grandmother made for you."

Suddenly Karen spoke, "It is blue like a summer sky." Then she realized Pippa had never seen the sky, and she felt bad. "I mean, I watched your grandmother make it. I. . . ." Karen stopped. She did not know what to say.

But Pippa reached over and ran her fingers up and down Karen's ugly pink corduroy jumper.

"I know what kind of material that is. It's corduroy, isn't it? It's so soft, a little like velvet. Grammy has taught me all about the different kinds of material." Then her fingers touched the little bunch of flowers pinned at the neckline. "Oh, you have flowers too. That must be very pretty. I love flowers." Then she turned to her grandmother, "Could you make me a jumper like Karen's, and with flowers too?" Then she turned to Karen and smiled, "We could be like twins."

"I believe I could do that," Mrs. Hooper said, "if Karen doesn't mind."

Karen tried to answer, but finally she whispered, "I don't mind." Then she had an idea. She unpinned the flowers on her jumper and placed them in Pippa's hands. "They will look pretty on your new corduroy jumper," she said. "We can both wear our jumpers to church next Sunday."

Pippa laughed, "Oh, that would be fun." Karen smiled too. It was hard to understand, but she felt as if she finally had Easter in her heart.

Spring, Spring, Stay Away

Marjorie Ellert Berg

Tim rubbed his eyes. A sliver of sunshine from under the window shade shone on his face. He yawned, shoved back the quilt, and climbed out of bed.

Pulling off his pajamas, Tim pushed them under the pillow. He tugged his jeans and sweatshirt on, then slipped on socks and shoes. He grabbed a corner of the quilt and pulled until most of the lumps smoothed out. *Looks OK,* he thought and bounded down the stairs, two at a time.

After glancing around the kitchen,

Tim headed for the back door. He was glad his mother wasn't there to make him eat breakfast right now. It was Saturday and he wanted to get out in his snow fort. After zipping his snowsuit, he slipped on boots and mittens. He dashed out the back door, but quickly slid to a halt, and frowned. The backyard had changed during the night. A gentle rain that had started before he went to bed had turned the fort into heaps of dirty snow.

Grabbing fistfuls of snow, Tim tried to pack it onto a crumbling wall. Soon his mittens became soggy, and the wall collapsed backward. The best fort that his friends, Mike and Joey, had ever helped him build was ruined—

gone forever. "I don't like spring," he grumbled, kicking at a pile of snow.

Feeling a growling hollowness in his stomach, Tim trudged back into the house and put away his snowsuit and boots.

His mother was watering tiny seedlings in pots and trays above the sink as Tim came into the kitchen. "Breakfast is almost ready," she said. "Will you set the table?"

After they finished their bowls of oatmeal and cups of milk, Tim helped clear the table. His mother laid out seed packets and then started drawing neat rectangles on graph paper, planning her garden.

"Spring is my favorite time of the year," she told Tim.

"Well, it's not mine," Tim replied. "There's nothing to do."

"You could ride your bike," his mother suggested. "Spring is a good bike-riding time."

"I don't want to ride my bike. I want to play in my fort!" Tim stomped off to his room. He climbed into the window seat and wrapped his arms around his knees.

Tim watched particles of dust dance in a strip of sunlight. They reminded him of snowflakes. He remembered playing with Mike and Joey in the fort. It had been a great place to play all winter. Now that the fort was gone, Mike and Joey might not want to play anymore.

As Tim shifted his knees, his elbow bumped the window shade. The shade whipped up with a slapping sound. Bright sunlight streamed into the room, and Tim felt warm. Leaning toward the window, he pushed it open. Soon the sunshine and fresh air made Tim tired. He closed his eyes and rested against the wall.

Before long, Tim heard voices outside. Opening his eyes, he looked down and saw Mike and Joey.

"I hope Tim can come over," Joey was saying, "My dad's building a tree house. I'll have a pole to slide down."

"Like the one we saw at the fire station?" Mike asked, excitedly.

"Exactly," Joey replied.

"Joey, I just saw your dad turn into your driveway," Mike shouted. "Let's find out if he's ready to start the tree-house."

Tim watched them run down the sidewalk. "A tree house," he said aloud. Joey's dad was building a tree house with a pole to slide down. And Joey wanted him to come over. Maybe he should go—just to watch, of course.

His mother was still working at the kitchen table when Tim walked in. "Can I go to Joey's?" he asked.

"Yes," his mother replied. Then she added, "You won't need your snow-suit, just a jacket. But put on your boots, because it's muddy."

Tim pulled his jacket from a hook and yanked on boots. His bike was in the garage. He could get to Joey's faster on a bike. After shoving the garage door up, Tim hopped on his bike and raced toward Joey's. The breeze felt good on his face. He had forgotten how much fun bike riding was.

Mike and Joey were helping Joey's dad stack boards in the garage. Tools and a sketch pad lay on the work bench.

Tim watched for a few moments. He thought about how Joey and Mike had helped build the snow fort. Then he asked, "Can I help?"

"You can bring the box of nails from the car," Joey's dad said, "and put them on the work bench."

When Tim set the box down, he glanced at the sketch pad. He saw a drawing of a treehouse on it. Steps went up one side, and a pole down the other. There were walls and a roof so they could play when it rained.

Maybe spring wouldn't be so bad, after all, Tim thought.

The Beast's Thorn
A Legend

After Jesus died, it is said that one of his disciples, Joseph of Arimathea, journeyed by sea and land to Glastonbury, in England. "I shall build a church here," he said, thrusting his staff into the ground. It was a piece of stick, blackened and smooth with age, yet it took root. It grew into a thorn tree of the same kind from which the Roman soldiers had made Christ's crown. Glastonbury became a holy shrine.

A young pilgrim whose name is forgotten, once set out to walk to Glastonbury from his village. "Bring back a holy relic for our church so that we may be blessed," said the villagers.

And when he returned with but a single black thorn they were disappointed. "It's no longer than your thumb nail!" they said in disgust. "It could have been picked from any farmer's hedge. Throw it away."

"Our Lord wore a crown of such thorns when he died," the pilgrim told them. "This is not an ordinary thorn."

Alas! It looked no different from the wayside thorns.

"Throw it away!" he was told again, and the people went back to their work.

The pilgrim did not throw the thorn away. He planted it at the end of the village and he tended it. The thorn grew into a small tree. "Soon it will blossom into white flowers," he told the villagers.

They were surprised that the tree had grown so quickly, but surely the young pilgrim had gone daft. Winter was then upon them. There would be no blossoms in the severe cold. And no matter how hard one searched, there was no sign of buds swelling on the hard bare twigs. "It will flower at Christmas," said the pilgrim.

"If it flowers at all it will be at Eastertide, with the Spring," they said.

Christmas came and went. The thorn was bare. The villagers had been right. Didn't they know about crops and other growing things?

The year ended and the new year began. The thorn tree stayed bare. Then came the Twelfth Night, the last day of the old Christmas holidays. And 12 days after Christmas the villagers went to sleep with never a thought for the thorn tree.

A pattering of feet woke them at midnight. Men jumped from their beds. Who was moving the cattle in the middle of the night? The clattering on the cobblestones sounded then like drum beats.

They flew to their windows. They stared down to the street. And what they saw there sent them struggling into clothes and dragging on boots.

The sheep! The cattle! Every beast that had been safely stalled at sundown, milled through the street, led by the great bull from the Manor House.

The village folk ran after their animals, a trail of people following, as far as the village end and the thorn tree.

The church clock struck midnight and the great lumbering bull from the Manor House sank to his knees on the frosted ground, before the tree. Sheep and cattle knelt behind him.

Then, one by one, the villagers knelt behind their animals in widening circles, ringing the tree—the thorn three, white with blossoms which glowed in the moonlight. Their pilgrim had brought them a blessing indeed from Glastonbury.

After that night, the tree was called the Beast's Thorn, as it was they who had sensed that the tree was different from a wayside tree. And the villagers told their children its story at Christmas time and at Easter, and now, you know it too.

The Sun Comes Dancing

Elizabeth Coatsworth

On Easter morn,
On Easter morn,
The sun comes dancing up the sky.

His light leaps up;
It shakes and swings,
Bewildering the dazzled eye.

On Easter morn
All earth is glad;
The waves rejoice in the bright sea.

Be still and listen
To your heart,
And hear it beating merrily!

Spring in the Woods

Sandra Liatsos

Wake up, woodchuck!
  Wake up, bear!
Stretch and yawn
  in April air.
Come outside.
  Prowl and play.
Spring is everywhere—
  TODAY!

An Easter Lily for Grandma

Mabel N. McCaw

Miss Frances was waiting for Tommy in her flower shop when he returned from his last delivery.

"Thank you, Tommy," she greeted him. "You worked well. There is one lily left, and it's for you."

"Oh! thank you," Tommy replied, going to look at the lily. "It's beautiful. I'll take it to the church for the Easter decorations tomorrow, and then it goes to my grandma."

"I am sure she will enjoy it," said Miss Frances.

"She will," Tommy said enthusiastically. "It's going to be a surprise, too."

Miss Frances started for the door of the shop. With the lily safely in his arms Tommy followed her, and they left the shop together.

Other people were already at the church the next morning when Tommy took his lily there. They, too, had brought lilies, and were placing them at the front of the church.

"Here comes Tommy. And here is just the place for his lily," Miss Carlson said. "Right here at the end of the first row."

"Thank you," said Tommy, as he handed his lily to Miss Carlson, "It does look good there. I'm taking it to Grandma after church."

Tommy thought the service that morning was especially good. The church was full. The choir sang its best, "Christ, the Lord, is risen today." The scent of the lilies filled the air, and the sunlight through the colored windows had never shined brighter. The day seemed perfect.

52

After the service was over, Tommy headed toward the front of the church to pick up his lily. On the way he met Mrs. Nelson, who was struggling with her lily and her cane.

"Here, let me carry that," Tommy offered.

"But you were going to get your own lily."

"That's all right. I'll help you get home first, and then I'll come back for it."

Fortunately Mrs. Nelson did not live far away, but their pace was slowed down because it was hard for her to walk. With the lily safely on Mrs. Nelson's table, Tommy hurried back to the church for his own lily plant. But where was it? The church was bare. All the lilies were gone!

To the nursing home, Tommy remembered. Lilies that were not picked up were to be taken to the nursing home in the neighborhood.

Quickly Tommy made for the door. He knew exactly where the home was located.

Out of breath he told a nurse at the desk why he had come.

"An Easter lily?" she asked. "Yes, several were brought here and given to our residents. I am afraid you are too late to get yours."

"But it's for my grandma," Tommy explained. "I have to have it."

"Well, you can try to get it back," the worker replied. "But I am not sure how."

She took Tommy down the hall to the residence section of the home. They looked in one room after another. He finally found it sitting on a table, in front of a woman in a wheel chair.

"Hello, Sarah," the nurse began, as she entered the room. "I have brought you a visitor. This is Tommy, to whom your lily belonged."

"And you gave it to me," Sarah said jubilantly. "It is the very first time anyone ever gave a lily to me. Thank you, thank you ever so much. Isn't it beautiful?"

"Yes, it is beautiful," Tommy agreed. "But you see. . . ."

"And you gave it to me, a person you have never known," Sarah interrupted. "That makes it even more beautiful."

Tommy looked helplessly at the nurse. There was no help there. He would have to try again. Perhaps it would help if he told Sarah about his grandmother.

"I have a grandmother like you," Tommy began.

"And you are giving her a lily, too," Sarah finished his sentence.

"I was, but, you see, a mistake has been made. I'm sorry, but. . . ."

"Sorry?" Sarah repeated. "Why be sorry when you have made me so happy?"

Tommy was silent. Sarah was right. How could one be sorry for bringing happiness to someone else? Sarah could keep the lily. He knew that somehow his grandmother would understand.

"That's all right," he said reaching down to squeeze Sarah's hands. "Have a happy Easter. Enjoy your lily."

"I will. I will, and thank you again," Sarah called after Tommy as he disappeared in the doorway.

That afternoon Tommy told his grandma what had happened. "I couldn't take the lily away from her, could I, Grandma? Not even to give to you."

"No, not even for me," Grandma answered. "You did what was right, Tommy. Maybe tomorrow you can take me over to meet Sarah, and we can enjoy our lily together."

"Oh! Grandma!" Tommy said, as he bent down and gave her a special Easter hug.

Leslie's Legacy

Linell Wohlers

Somebody's lilacs are in bloom," said Leslie's mother.

Leslie closed her eyes and drew in a breath of sweet spring air. It was great to relax in the backyard for the first picnic of the year after a long, cold winter! Now after a few weeks of warm sunshine, the songs of birds filled the air. Leaves and grass were green, and flowers were blooming.

Suddenly Leslie felt something tickly crawling up her lavender pants leg.

"Mom, look!" she exclaimed. "A butterfly is on me!"

"What pretty markings!" said her mother.

"I hope it stays a while so we can look at it," said Leslie.

The butterfly seemed to be trying to crawl under Leslie's leg into the shadow. It kept falling over as it crawled.

"It seems so fragile," said Leslie. "Maybe I should help it fly again."

Carefully, she put a finger under the butterfly's tickly legs and held it up to the warm spring breeze. But the butterfly wobbled and couldn't seem to move its wings. Finally it lost its grip altogether and fell from Leslie's finger. It walked a little way into her shadow again.

"It must like me," Leslie smiled. "It doesn't want to leave."

"Maybe it's resting," said her mother.

After a while, the butterfly lay very still with its wing folded together. Leslie couldn't get it to crawl onto her finger anymore. Its tickly feet were all folded inward. Occasionally its wings stirred in the breeze like a delicate piece of paper, but the butterfly itself did not move.

"What happened?" cried Leslie, in alarm. "It won't move!"

"I think it just died," said her mother.

A tear slid down Leslie's cheek, and she cried very softly.

"Most butterflies don't live very long," said her mother. "They go through the miracle of changing from a caterpillar to a butterfly. Then they live a few days, lay eggs, and die. Their lives are colorful and interesting—but short."

"It's not fair," said Leslie, "that they die so fast."

"It seems sad to you, Leslie," said her mother. "But I think it's special that this butterfly wanted to die here."

"By me?" said Leslie.

"Yes," said her mother. "I think they usually crawl off to die under a bush or hide in a clump of weeds where no one ever notices them."

"Or worse yet," said Leslie, "some of them get smashed against the front of the car." She remembered how sorry she had felt, seeing the butterflies on the grille of their car after a long drive. Their wings had been crushed and ruined. This butterfly died undamaged and perfect.

"Maybe this butterfly wanted me to have its wings after it died," said Leslie.

"Of course!" said her mother. "Its legacy to you."

"What's a legacy?" asked Leslie.

"Before people die, they often write in a will that they want something special given to a certain person who will appreciate it. Like when Grandma Frederickson died, she left me her beautiful old necklace."

"So when this butterfly died, it left me its wings," said Leslie.

"I think so," said her mother. "You can keep the wings for a long time. When you look at them in summer, you can think how they flew, bringing a little color and magic from the flowers up into the sky! When you look at them in winter, you can remember when they were folded in their dark chrysalis, waiting for spring."

"When I look at them anytime, I will think that this butterfly picked me to land on," said Leslie.

There Is a Green Hill Far Away

Cecil F. Alexander

There is a green hill far away,
Outside a city wall,
Where the dear Lord was crucified,
Who died to save us all.

We may not know, we cannot tell,
What pains he had to bear,
But we believe it was for us
He hung and suffered there.

He died that we might be forgiv'n;
He died to make us good,
That we might go at last to heav'n,
Saved by his precious blood.

Jason's Egg Hunt

Gay Bell

Jason opened the barn door as quietly as he could. He peeked inside. Were there Easter eggs hidden in the barn? At first glance he didn't see any, but they could be hidden in the hay.

Jason had looked forward to the Easter egg hunt all week.

Now he was feeling sad and disappointed. There wasn't *one* Easter egg in his basket.

He'd spotted a red egg in the tall grass next to the house and a blue egg under the bottom board of the pig pen. But every time he raced to pick up an egg, his sister or his brother got there first.

Alex shouldn't have run so fast! Jason thought angrily. *And Millie should have helped! I saw the egg in the apple tree before she did, but I couldn't reach it. It's not fair!*

Jason knew that when he went back to the house, their father would make Alex and Millie give him some of their eggs. But he wanted to find his *own* Easter eggs!

He watched his brother and sister dashing around the farmyard. All at once, he realized that Alex and Millie had forgotten to look for eggs inside the barn!

I bet I'll find lots of Easter eggs in the barn, Jason thought excitedly. He gripped the handle of his basket and raced to the empty horse stall. He hunted through the straw.

There was nothing there.

Jason ran to look behind the hay bales. Not one Easter egg. *I know there are eggs hidden in this barn!* he thought. *I just know there are.* Jason looked all around. Suddenly, he thought of the perfect place.

He dashed to the ladder that led to the hay loft. Holding his basket tightly, he climbed up the ladder.

The light was dim in the loft. He'd have to look hard to find the Easter eggs. Carefully he started to search through the hay. But just then, he heard a funny noise. He crawled over to the corner under the eaves.

"Cluck!" It was a familiar sound. Jason groped around the hay. He touched something fluffy and soft. It was Molly, his pet Rhode Island hen.

"Molly!" Jason stroked her soft feathers. "I've been worried about you. You didn't come when I put out your grain."

Molly stood up. She rolled something over with her beak.

"Hey!" Jason whispered excitedly. He crouched closer to get a better look. Then his shoulders slumped, and he sighed. It wasn't an Easter egg, as he'd thought. Just a plain old brown egg.

He started to turn away. But at that moment, he heard a loud peeping noise. It was coming from inside the egg!

Jason looked at the egg closely. He saw a small hole in the shell.

"Peck! Peck!" A crack appeared next to the hole. Soon the shell was broken all around.

Jason could see a baby chick inside!

The baby chick gave a kick with its feet, popped out of the shell, and flopped on its stomach.

Molly clucked loudly.

Jason held his breath.

The baby chick rested. Then it struggled to its feet. Bits of fluff floated around the chick as its feathers dried.

Molly clucked softly.

The small bundle of new life started to peep. It hopped toward Molly.

Jason scrambled down the ladder.

"Dad! Millie! Alex!" Jason shouted at the top of his voice. "Come see the Easter egg *I* found!"

Elena's Ciambella   Anna Milo Upjohn

As Elena scampered over the road, the town clock struck a quarter to four. Elena had an important engagement. Her mother had sent her to draw a jar of water from the public well outside the town, and on the way back she was to stop at the bakery to get her *ciambella*, which was to come out of the oven at four.

A *ciambella* is an Easter cake, but it is different from any other cake in the world. It is made of flour and sugar and olive oil, and tastes like a crisp cooky. If you are a girl, yours will be in the form of a dove; if a boy, in the form of a galloping horse, with a handle of twisted dough from mane to tail to carry it by. Whichever it may be, an Easter egg will be baked inside the *ciambella*, and the cake will be stuck full of downy feathers which wave and look festive.

Elena's cake was an unusually large one, in the shape of a dove, of course, with wings and tail feathers and an open beak. It had been brought to the bakery on a tray by Elena's mother, and left to be baked.

As Elena panted up the hill she saw Giuseppa outside the *cabane*, or hut, helping her mother with the washing. The baby stood in a high, narrow box where he could look on and yet was out of mischief, and there he waved his arms and shouted with excitement as the suds flew.

"Where are you going?" called Giuseppa as Elena passed.

"To get my *ciambella*," cried Elena. "Have you got yours?"

Giuseppa shook her head. "I'm not going to have any," she said.

"Not this year," added her mother, looking up. "Perhaps next. But we are going to make the *cabane* clean for Easter."

Elena looked at Giuseppa sympathetically.

"Too bad!" exclaimed Elena. "Well, I must hurry. *Ciao* [a parting that is pronounced "chow" and means good-bye], Giuseppa."

"*Ciao*, Elena."

When Elena reached the bakery she found a great crowd there. The four-o'clock cakes were coming out of the oven. Far back in the row Elena could see her own *ciambella* on the stone floor of the oven, larger than all the rest, its feathers waving tantalizingly in the heat.

In the midst of the women and children stood the cook, with smooth, black hair and huge earrings of gold and pearls, which reached to her shoulders, and with a clean, flowered kerchief tucked into her corset. She was bare-armed and brown, and held what looked like a great pancake turner with a very long handle. With this she could reach into the depths of the oven, which was as big as a pantry, and scoop out the cakes, even those all the way back.

There were all sorts of cakes, large and small; some were cookies, and some were big loaves made with almonds and honey and eggs. The whole place smelled delicious, and everyone stood on tiptoe to see his own cake pulled out of the oven. Finally Elena's *ciambella* was put into her hands, still hot and fragrant, though she had waited for it to cool somewhat on a tray.

Just then a little girl named Letitia came in to ask for coals with which to light the fire at home. The cook raked a few from the oven and put them into the pot of ashes that Letitia carried. Covering them with her apron, Letitia went out with Elena.

"Just look at my *ciambella*," said Elena proudly, as she carried it carefully in both hands. "Isn't it a beauty!"

"Yes," said Letitia. "I am going to have one, too. It will be baked tomorrow. Of course," she added, "it won't be quite as big as yours, because Maria will have one, and Gino will have a horse. But they'll all taste the same."

"Just think," said Elena, "Giuseppa isn't going to have any at all!"

"Not any?" cried Letitia. "How dreadful! I never heard of a house without a *ciambella*! They must be very poor."

"Yes, but at school Giuseppa always has a clean apron and clean hands. She helps her mother a lot too. Well, *ciao*, Letitia."

"*Ciao*, Elena."

The girls parted, and Elena walked proudly through the streets, carrying the cake as though in a procession.

She climbed the outside stair which led to her house, built over the donkey stable. Her mother had gone out to the fountain to polish her pots. The big dim room, with its brown rafters and the dark furniture arranged along the walls, was very quiet.

A patch of sunshine made a bright spot on the stone floor, and in it a white pigeon drowsed. It did not move, even when Elena stepped over it. The little girl looked down and laughed at the comical resemblance between the pigeon and her *ciambella*; but her own pigeon sat up very straight and stiff, because it had an Easter egg baked inside it.

Elena set the cake carefully on a big chest while she struggled to open the bottom drawer of the bureau. There she laid the cake in a nest of clean aprons and handkerchiefs, to rest until Saturday afternoon, when it would be taken out to be blessed. Not until Sunday morning would its fine feathers be plucked and its crisp wings bitten off.

The *ciambella* safely lodged in a drawer, Elena climbed on a chair and got a piece of bread and some sheep's cheese from the cupboard; then she ran to find her mother.

The next days were very busy. Everyone in Sezze was cleaning house frantically before Easter. Washing hung over every balcony, the yellow and flowered handkerchiefs and aprons making the whole street gay. Every bit of furniture was polished, windows were cleaned, curtains washed and floors scrubbed. Above all, the copper water jars and basins were taken out to the fountains and scoured with lemon and sand until they shone like red gold.

There was the warmth of spring in the air after a cold winter. On the slopes below the town the almond trees were in blossom, and the snow had disappeared from the mountains, the tops of which were drifted with clouds.

Far below the town a fertile plain—the Pontine Marshes—stretched out to the sea. Giuseppa's father worked on the flats, and the family lived in a *cabane*, but it was high up on the mountain, just below the town, where land was cheap. It was true that Giuseppa's father was very poor, but he was also saving his money to build a little stone house to take the place of the *cabane*. He told the children that when they had a house they should also have a *ciambella* every year.

In the meantime Giuseppa helped her mother make the *cabane* as neat as possible for Easter. It was a poor place indeed; round, with a thatched roof which came to a peak at the top. Inside there was only one room, and that had an earthen floor and no windows. There were no openings except the doors, and no chimney.

When the fire was built on the floor in the middle of the room, the smoke struggled up through holes in the roof; but the family lived out in the sun most of the time, and went into the *cabane* only when it rained or was very cold.

As Elena went back and forth for water those busy days, she sometimes looked over the wall and saw Giuseppa hanging clothes on the bushes or beating a mattress; and there was smoke coming through the roof as if water were being heated. Elena felt very sorry for Giuseppa, and every night prayed to God to send her a *ciambella*.

Giuseppa, not knowing this, felt bitter toward Elena and jealous of her great feathered cake. Also she herself prayed earnestly for a *ciambella*. On Easter morning she made herself as fine as she could and went to church. She combed back her short hair and laid a white embroidered handkerchief over it. She had small gold earrings and a coral necklace, and she put on a light blue cotton apron and her corn-colored handkerchief with roses over her shoulders.

On her way home Elena came running after her. "Oh, Giuseppa," she asked earnestly, "did you get a *ciambella*?"

"No, I didn't," said Giuseppa, and passed on.

Elena was much disappointed. She had prayed hard, and felt that a cake should have been sent to Giuseppa. Then suddenly she stopped short in the street. "Why," she said, "perhaps God hasn't got a *ciambella*, and I have!"

She went home thoughtfully and opened the drawer and looked a long time at her *ciambella*. Then she ate her dinner of boiled chicken and artichokes fried in batter. After dinner Elena took the cake lovingly in her arms and carried it onto the street. It was the last time it would be on parade. She passed the groups of children, all munching *ciambella*, and made her way to Giuseppa's hut. Giuseppa was outside, feeding the baby from a bowl of bread and milk.

"Happy Easter!" cried Elena.

"Happy Easter!" replied Giuseppa, her eyes fixed on the cake.

"I brought my *ciambella* to eat with you," said Elena cautiously, "and you may hold it, and oh, Giuseppa, you may have the egg!"

Giuseppa grew scarlet. "I never saw such a beauty," she said. "And what feathers!"

"I stuck them into the dough myself," said Elena. "That is why there are so many."

"Do you know," said Giuseppa shyly, "I prayed for a *ciambella*."

"And you got it!" cried Elena triumphantly.

Dandelions for Dinner

Helen Mallmann

"Oh, yuck," said Trevor, wrinkling his nose. He watched his dad set a bowl of salad on the kitchen table. What's that dark green stuff?"

"Endive," said his father.

"Yuck," said Trevor.

"You've never even tasted endive," said Sarah, Trevor's older sister. "You always say yuck. How do you know you don't like things unless you try them?"

"What difference does it make if I don't eat everything?" asked Trevor. "I won't starve."

"You might want to go somewhere some day," his father said, "and you won't be able to because you refuse to eat anything new."

Trevor felt the corners of his mouth turn down. He stuck out his lower lip and frowned.

"Xiong, you sit here, next to Trevor," his mother said to Trevor's new friend. "I'm glad you can have dinner with us tonight." She set bowls of spaghetti and sauce on the table.

"Oh, good!" said Trevor. "We're having spaghetti. I love spaghetti." He sat down next to Xiong.

"You said yuck to spaghetti before you tried it," said Sarah.

After Trevor's father asked God's blessing on the food, he used a tongs to put spaghetti on his plate. "Have you ever eaten spaghetti, Xiong?" he asked, passing the bowl to him.

"No," said Xiong. He used the tongs to put some spaghetti on his plate.

Trevor stared at Xiong as he took the bowl from him. "You'll like it," said Trevor, a little worried that he might not. "It's good."

The spaghetti sauce was passed and then the salad. "The small bowl is for your salad," said Trevor's father, putting some in his bowl and passing it to Xiong.

Xiong put some in his bowl and passed the bowl to Trevor.

"Yuck," said Trevor and passed the salad to his mother.

"Quit saying yuck," said Sarah.

As they were eating, Trevor's father asked Xiong, "How do you like the spaghetti?"

"It's good," said Xiong. "I like the salad, too. The endive tastes like dandelion greens."

"Dandelion greens!" exclaimed Trevor. "Do you eat dandelion greens?"

"Sure," said Xiong. "Right now they taste the best. The flower hasn't come on yet. My mother digs them every spring at the park near the soccer field."

"What time is your soccer practice?" Trevor's mother asked.

"At 6:30," answered Trevor.

"We have plenty of time," said his father. "We'll take our bikes."

"Did you ask your parents about soccer camp?" Xiong asked.

"I sure did!" said Trevor. "But Dad says he has to talk to the coach."

After dinner Trevor and Xiong helped clear the table and put the dishes into the dishwasher.

"Soccer camp will be fun," Xiong exclaimed. "I hope you can go!"

"I hope so, too!" said Trevor.

Trevor and his father and Xiong rode their bikes to the soccer field. They walked over to talk to the coach.

"Xiong is going to soccer camp," said Trevor's father. "Trevor wants to go, too. Can you tell me about it?"

"Sure," said the coach. "It's out at Camp Flying Eagle right after school's out in June. This year we're taking the kids out on Monday morning, and they'll be staying until Friday afternoon. We think these kids can handle being away from home that long, especially if they have a good buddy with them."

Xiong looked at Trevor.

"There's one thing, though," the

coach went on. "The kids have to eat what the cooks put on the table. We serve good, nutritious food because we want the kids to know what it's like to be 'in training.' There's no snack bar out there."

"Thanks," said Trevor's father.

The coach blew his whistle, and the kids out on the field ran to gather around him.

Trevor felt something sink inside of him. He looked at his father. He felt the corners of his mouth turn down. "You're going to let me go aren't you?" he asked.

With a twinkle in his eye, his father grinned and said, "Well, I couldn't let you go if I thought you were going to starve out there, could I?"

After soccer practice they rode their bikes to Xiong's house.

Xiong's mother came to the door. "It was nice of you to invite Xiong for dinner today," she called to Trevor and his father.

"We enjoyed having him," said Trevor's father.

Xiong carried his bike up the porch steps and leaned it on the house. He said something quietly to his mother.

"Sure," said Xiong's mother. "Ask him."

Xiong came down the steps and said to Trevor, "My mother says I can invite you for dinner tomorrow. Can you come?"

Trevor looked at his father. "Can I?" he asked.

"Sure, Trevor," his father said.

The next day after school Trevor and Xiong pedaled their bikes to Xiong's house.

"Something wrong?" Xiong asked. "You haven't said much all day."

"Well, not exactly," answered Trevor.

They went into the house. Dinner was ready. Xiong's brothers and his sister were standing around the dining room table. There were chopsticks for Xiong's parents to eat with, but the children had forks.

"My father has to be at work at 5:00, so we eat early," explained Xiong.

Xiong's mother set a platter of egg rolls and a bowl of salad on the table.

"I love egg rolls," said Xiong as he sat down next to Trevor.

Xiong's father said the table prayer. He picked up the platter of egg rolls and put two on his plate.

"Have you ever eaten egg rolls, Trevor?" asked Xiong's father, passing the platter to him.

Yuck, thought Trevor. *How did I get into this?* Then he remembered what his dad had said about wanting to go somewhere. He couldn't go to soccer camp unless he would try new foods.

"No," said Trevor. Slowly he put an egg roll on his plate and passed the platter to Xiong.

Xiong smiled at Trevor. "You'll like it. They're good," said Xiong.

Xiong's father picked up the salad bowl. "The small bowl is for your salad," he said, putting some in his salad bowl.

As Trevor put some salad in his bowl, he saw some dandelion greens mixed with the other salad greens. He passed the salad to Xiong. Trevor jabbed his fork into the salad.

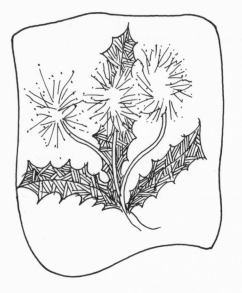

I have to eat this, he said to himself. He put it into his mouth. After chewing it a little, he swallowed it. He broke off a piece of egg roll with the side of his fork and put it into his mouth. As he chewed it, his eyes opened wide.

Trevor looked at Xiong. He had been watching.

"How do you like it?" asked Xiong.

"It's good," said Trevor. Grinning, he added, "Soccer camp's going to be fun."

At Easter Time

Margaret Hillert

All in the first glad days of spring
I'll set about my Eastering.
Up hill, down hollow,
Quick to follow
Where rabbits caper in a ring
Under the moon.

And soon,
After moonset and sunrise,
I'll turn my eyes
To speckled eggs and birds newborn,
Cradled by song in the early morn;
And after sudden showers
Taste flowers wet with rain.

Then,
When the bells of Easter ring,
And Easter choirs sing,
I'll take my place,
Cathedral windows rainbowed on my face.

Grandma Hinkle to the Rescue!

Alan Cliburn

Grandma Hinkle was sweeping her walk the Saturday afternoon before Easter when Lisa and Johnny raced up to her.

"You've got to help us, Grandma Hinkle!" Lisa exclaimed.

"You're our last resort!" Johnny added, breathing hard.

Grandma Hinkle, who was their friend and not really their grandmother at all, smiled. "Well, I'll certainly help if I can. What seems to be the problem?"

"Tomorrow's Easter," Lisa began.

"And the store ran out of Easter egg dye," Johnny continued.

"Do you have any we could borrow?" Lisa asked.

"It's real important," Johnny said. "The judging starts at four o'clock!"

"What judging is that?" Grandma Hinkle wanted to know.

"They're having a contest at the park to pick the prettiest eggs," Lisa told her impatiently. "Do you have any dye?"

"No, I never use it," Grandma Hinkle answered.

"Well, do you have any food coloring?" Johnny asked. "Mom said that might work."

"I'm afraid not," Grandma Hinkle replied.

"There goes the contest then," Lisa said sadly.

"It's our own fault for waiting 'til the last minute," Johnny decided. "Thanks anyway, Grandma Hinkle. Come on, Lisa."

"Wait just a minute," Grandma Hinkle called after them. "I don't have any Easter egg dye, but I can still help you color your eggs. We didn't have fancy store-bought dyes when I was growing up, you know, but we still had beautiful eggs at Easter."

Lisa and Johnny looked at each other. "How?" Lisa wanted to know.

"What did you use for the coloring?" Johnny asked.

"Run home and get your eggs," Grandma Hinkle suggested. "I'll show you."

A few minutes later Lisa and Johnny were inside Grandma Hinkle's kitchen, watching as she placed the eggs into a large kettle of cold water.

"Wouldn't it be faster if the water was boiling when you put the eggs in?" Lisa asked. "Mother says they should be hardboiled before we color them."

"Yes, they should be," Grandma Hinkle agreed. "But if you put a cold egg into boiling water, it will usually crack. If they both heat together, there should be no cracking."

"I still don't see how you can color eggs without Easter egg dye," Johnny said.

"You will," Grandma Hinkle promised. "Lisa, run into the back yard and pick some flowers."

"Well, OK," Lisa replied, giving her brother a look.

"And you come with me," Grandma Hinkle told Johnny.

"OK," he agreed, shrugging as she started down the steps to the cellar.

It was cool and dark in the cellar. Grandma Hinkle led the way to a large crate of brown onions. "Just remove the outer skins," she instructed. "Like this." Johnny watched as she easily peeled off the outer brown layer of onion skin. "We'll need enough to fill this little kettle."

While Johnny gathered the onion skins, Grandma Hinkle went back to the kitchen to check on the eggs. Soon Lisa came through the back door with an armful of flowers. "Is this enough?" she asked.

"Plenty," Grandma Hinkle said. "And what a lovely assortment! Separate them by colors."

"OK, I got the onion skins," Johnny said, coming up from the cellar.

Lisa wrinkled her nose. "Onion skins! What are they for?"

"You'll see," Grandma Hinkle told her with a laugh. Quickly she added water to the kettle of onion skins and placed it on the stove. "The eggs should be ready for coloring and decorating in a few minutes."

"Decorating?" Johnny repeated. "How? And with what?"

"Just wait and see," Grandma Hinkle replied, stirring the onion skins.

Grandma Hinkle lifted an egg out of the boiling water with her tongs and dipped just one end of the egg into the kettle of simmering onion skins. She held the egg in place for a few seconds, then lifted it out.

"It's orange!" Lisa exclaimed.

"Yes, and the longer I leave it in, the darker it will get," Grandma Hinkle explained. "The onion skins made a kind of dye."

"And will the flowers make dye, too?" Johnny asked.

"Some will," Grandma Hinkle told him, "but most of mine won't. They can be used in another way, though. In fact, in two other ways! Let me show you."

She placed some purple iris petals into a small saucepan and heated them for a few seconds. Then, as Lisa and Johnny watched, she wrapped the eggs in the purple petals.

"We'll let this set for a while," she said. "And then you'll see that we have a lovely pale purple Easter egg! That's one way of doing it. When I was a little girl, we used to paste the petals on, too, for decoration."

"Should I run home and get some paste?" Johnny asked.

"We can make our own," Grandma Hinkle decided. "Just a little flour and water will do fine."

After she mixed the paste, Grandma Hinkle began decorating an egg with various colored petals—red, pink, yellow, and purple. She started at the middle and worked her way down, leaving the top of the egg showing.

"That looks neat!" Johnny exclaimed. "Can I try one?"

"Me, too," Lisa said. "But I want to dip mine in the onion dye first so it'll be orange."

For the next hour Lisa and Johnny decorated eggs, dipping some in the onion dye, wrapping some in purple iris petals, and pasting tiny petals on others.

"Oh, no, look at the time!" Lisa shrieked suddenly. "We're due at the park in 10 minutes!"

Johnny grinned. "I'm having so much fun that I don't care if I go to the park or not!"

"Yes, but I want the other kids to see our eggs," Lisa said, putting hers in a basket.

"Me, too," Johnny decided, getting up from the table. "Thanks a lot, Grandma Hinkle."

"You really came to the rescue," Lisa added.

"I was glad to help," Grandma Hinkle said with a smile. "See you at church tomorrow. Happy Easter!"

"Happy Easter!" Lisa and Johnny called together as they hurried out the back door with their baskets of eggs, colored and decorated the old-fashioned way.

Closet Cleaning Reward

Margaret Shauers

Todd picked up his big, yellow dump truck and walked toward the door. "I am glad it's finally springtime," he told his mother. "It's nice out today and I'm going to play with Mark."

"Oh, oh," said his mother. "I had hoped you would help me clean the spare bedroom today."

"Do I have to?" Todd asked. "Mark and I want to build a sand castle in his backyard. I was taking my truck to haul the sand."

"Can't you build it this afternoon?" she asked. "If you will carry things to the trash barrel and the attic, it will really help me."

"Well . . . ," Todd said, "only Grandma used the spare bedroom at Christmas. It can't be very dirty."

Mother laughed. "It's dirty enough. And you know how we store everything in that closet. That's what I really want to clean."

Todd looked at the dump truck. It would be a lot more fun mixing sand with water to build a sand castle than it would be cleaning a closet. But last Christmas the closet had been so full of boxes that there had hardly been room for Grandma's dresses.

"I'll help," he said and put down his truck. "But let's start right now. Mark and I have a lot of work to do too."

Todd's mother nodded. Moments later she had the door of the spare bedroom closet open and the first box out.

Closet cleaning wasn't as bad as Todd had feared. For one thing, his mother kept pulling out the funniest things—a long skinny dress she'd had before she and Daddy were married, a baby rattle, and a tiny red shirt Todd couldn't believe he'd ever been small enough to wear. She found some good stuff, too, like the old football helmet of Daddy's that Todd was sure he could wear in another year.

Finally, his mother pulled out the last box. It seemed heavy. "Now, what can this be?" she said. Then, as she opened the lid and Todd looked inside, she exclaimed, "Why this is leftover from that course in sandpainting I took years ago. The colors are all mixed together. I guess you may as well throw it away."

Todd looked again at the pearly pink, blue, and silver sand. "Colored sand would make great designs on our sand castle," he said. "May I have it? Please?"

His mother handed him the box. "You are welcome to it, Todd, and thank you for your help," she said. "With you to carry things away as I took them out, there's nothing left to do but scrub the floor. And I don't need your help for that. Why don't you go to Mark's now? I'll call you for lunch."

Todd looked out the window at the beautiful, sunshiny day. "Thanks," he said, smiling. "I'm glad I helped." Then he turned and ran down the hall to get his truck. He knew Mark would be as happy as he was with his closet cleaning reward!

In God's Protecting Goodness Trust

A European Legend Retold by Ron and Lyn Klug

Many years ago a tiny village lay hidden in the mountains of Europe. The kind people of the village lived in simple cottages, ate vegetables and black bread, and drank goat's milk.

One day Katrin, a young girl of the village, was tending her family's goats on the slopes of the mountains. Late in the afternoon she came running down to her home, shouting, "Mama, come quickly. Up on the mountain I found a woman and two children. They are very tired and hungry, and the woman asked me to bring her something to eat."

Although they had little themselves, Katrin's mother filled a jar with goat's milk and wrapped some bread and cheese in a cloth. Then she followed Katrin back up the mountain.

As they came around a bend in the path, they saw a woman sitting on a rock under a beech tree. On her lap was a little girl, as beautiful as she, and not far away a little dark-eyed boy played quietly. Nearby an old man was unloading a mule, preparing to camp for the night.

"This is strange," Katrin's mother said. "These people are dressed in expensive clothes such as only the rich wear. Yet they ask food from poor people like us." Still, she offered the bread and cheese and milk.

"Thank you, you are very kind," the woman said. And she gave the food to her daughter Erika and her son Alex, and to the old man, who was their servant Kuno.

"Tell me about your village," the beautiful woman said to Katrin's mother.

When she learned that the villagers were kind and that strangers almost never entered the hidden valley, she exclaimed, "I think God must have sent me here! I have been driven from my home, and I need a safe place where we can live in peace."

The four strangers followed Katrin and her mother down into the valley. There the woman rented a vacant house and hired a village girl named Marie to be her servant.

Early the next morning the woman gave Marie a silver coin and said, "Go, buy us some eggs for breakfast."

"You mean the eggs of the little birds who sing in the forest?" Marie asked in amazement.

"No, of course not," the woman said, smiling. "I mean eggs from chickens."

"I don't know what chickens are," Marie replied.

Then the woman remembered that this was a village deep in the mountains. Chickens' eggs had just come to Europe from Asia, and only the wealthy people in the cities could buy them. She sent old Kuno to the city across the mountains.

A few days later Kuno returned with a large wooden cage containing two roosters and six hens. Katrin and all her friends gathered to look at these strange new birds.

Months passed. Autumn came, and winter. Still the woman and her children lived among the people of the village. The woman was generous and shared her money with the villagers. In return they brought her game they had hunted and helped her in any way they could. When spring came, the children of the village hurried to the forest and picked violets and lilies to bring back to the woman and her children.

On the day before Easter the woman was thinking, "The people of the village have been so kind to me. I would like to make them happy, but what can I do?" She couldn't give a big party, because there was little food to be had in the village. She couldn't give them presents, because there were none to buy. All she had were eggs, and that wouldn't be much of a treat, she thought. But suddenly she had an idea. She called Marie, her maid.

They went to the woods and gathered roots and moss and berries. With these they dyed some eggs—pink and blue and green and orange and lilac. They used other eggs to bake cakes and custards.

Late that afternoon Alex and Erika went through the village stopping at every cottage. "We would like to invite you to an Easter party at our house tomorrow," they said. "Come right after the church service."

Everyone looked forward to the party. On Easter morning they all put on the best clothes they had, and after church, a long line of people stretched from the church to the home of Alex and Erika.

The woman met the villagers at the door and led them to her garden where long tables were set up. She told the parents to sit down, but to the children she said, "Go into the woods with Alex and Erika. Make little nests of moss and hide them under the trees—only remember where you left them."

The children all ran off to the woods, laughing and shouting.

The parents sat down to a feast of eggs—boiled eggs, fried eggs, omelets, and custards. Because the people had never had eggs before, they thought they were wonderful.

When the children came back from the woods, they too enjoyed a feast of eggs. They did not even notice when Alex, Erika, and Kuno slipped off into the woods.

After the meal the woman said, "Children, go back to the woods and look for your nests."

Soon happy cries could be heard as each child found a nest filled with brightly colored eggs. They brought these back to their parents, who found a saying written on each egg:

In God's protecting goodness trust,
For God will help the kind and just.

That evening, as the kind woman said good-bye to the last of the villagers, she saw a young man carrying a bundle come down the mountain path. He looked sad and tired, so she called him and asked him where he was going.

"I am on my way to the next village to see my mother, who is old and sick," he said. "I am very hungry because the little money I have I am saving for my mother."

The woman gave him something to eat, and as he was about to leave, she handed him a gold piece and some eggs for his mother.

Refreshed, the young peasant continued on his way. As he walked along the narrow trail, he came across a horse wearing a saddle and bridle and tied to a tree. "That's strange," the young man thought. "I wonder if someone is hurt and needs help."

He looked down into a ravine, and there he saw a man dressed in armor, lying still on the ground. The young man scrambled down the rocks, pulled off the knight's helmet, and used it as a dipper to get some water from a stream nearby. When he poured the water over the knight's face, the man opened his eyes. "Thank God for sending you," he murmured. "I fell down into this ravine, and I was afraid I would die here. I was too weak to move."

The young man remembered the eggs he was going to give his mother. He peeled one and carefully fed it to the knight.

As the young peasant was about to peel the second egg, the knight saw the saying written on the egg:

In God's protecting goodness trust,
For God will help the kind and just.

"Stop!" the knight cried. "Let me have the egg just as it is, and I will give you a gold piece for it."

Amazed, the young peasant exchanged the egg for the gold piece. Then he helped the knight to the village where his mother lived. There a doctor told the knight, "You will have to stay in bed for six weeks."

"Oh, no!" groaned the knight. "My master has been waiting for news of her for so long!"

Nevertheless, like a good soldier, he obeyed.

Meanwhile the kind woman and her two children continued to live in the village. Once again the servant Kuno went to the city across the mountains. When he returned, he looked sad and worried. "Madam, I have bad news for you," he said.

They talked together for a long time. Then Kuno went to the mayor of the village, who was also the miller, and said, "My mistress wants to talk with you."

The mayor came to the home of the woman, who told him this story: "I am Rosalinde, daughter of the duke. In my father's court there were two knights, Klaus and Frederick. Both wanted to marry me. I chose Frederick. Klaus was very angry and threatened to get revenge.

"Frederick and I were married and lived happily for a long time. We had the two children, Erika and Alex. Then the Emperor sent my husband to Palestine to fight in the Crusades, leaving me alone with the children."

While Frederick was away, Klaus said that unless I married him, he would put me and the children into prison. Then he brought many men and began to attack our castle. My servant Kuno knew a secret passage and helped us escape. But today along the road he saw Klaus, who was stopping at every village asking if anyone had seen a woman and two children. I'm afraid that if he comes to this village, people will tell him I'm here."

"Don't be afraid," the mayor said. "The villagers will not tell the evil man that you are here. And if he comes to capture you, we will defend you with our lives."

Then the mayor went to every cottage in the village and told the story of Lady Rosalinde.

The next day when Klaus came along asking about Rosalinde, the villagers all pretended to know nothing.

"She is not here," Klaus said, and he and his men went away.

After that, Lady Rosalinde again lived in peace in the village. Every evening she and Erika and Alex went to the little church in the village and prayed that God would bring Frederick safely back from Palestine.

One evening in May, just as they were leaving the church, a stranger came by, wearing a long cloak. The top half of his face was hidden by a hood, and the bottom, by a flowing white beard. He asked the children what they were doing.

"We have been praying for the safe return of our father," Alex replied.

Lady Rosalinde grew afraid that the stranger might carry news of them to Klaus. But suddenly the stranger threw back his hood and pulled off his false beard—and a young handsome knight stood before them.

"Frederick!" Lady Rosalinde cried and rushed to his side.

"Father!" Erika and Alex shouted and threw themselves into his arms.

"How did you find us?" Lady Rosalinde asked.

"I found you because you are so kind and good." He explained how he had returned to find his castle ruined. "I learned how Klaus had tried to capture you," he said. "I sent my men to search the land for you, but none could bring me any news. One man did not return for a long time, and I was afraid he had been killed. But after six weeks he came back with a strange story and a colored egg. On it, in your writing, was the motto of my family:

In God's protecting goodness trust,
For God will help the kind and just.

Then Frederick explained how, disguised as an old man, he learned that Rosalinde and the children were in the hidden valley.

Rosalinde and the children brought Frederick into the village, and all the people welcomed him warmly.

Frederick thanked the people for their kindness to his family and said, "Now, dear friends, to show you how grateful I am, I promise to give a fine big cow to every family in the village. And every year at Easter time, Rosalinde and I will send colored eggs to the children, not only in this village, but throughout the kingdom."

Then Lord Frederick and his family returned to their home, rebuilt their castle, and lived happily there. But they never forgot the kind people in the hidden valley, and every year they sent them colored eggs.

As years passed, the custom spread from country to country, until now colored eggs are given at Easter time in many lands.

The Easter Basket

Sandra Liatsos

I saw an Easter basket
resting in a tree.
It held three lovely
light blue eggs,
but they were not for me.
A mother robin
fluttered down
and landed on the nest.
She sat upon
those three blue eggs
and sang her Easter best.

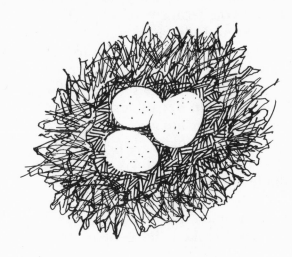

Let's Celebrate

Jacqueline Rowland

I think I'd like to beat a drum
When the first pussy willows come,
Or shoot off rockets in the air,
When springtime signs are everywhere:
A host of dandelions, golden bright,
A little bud, all green and tight,
A robin with a bit of string—
I'd love to shout then, "Happy spring!"
Then bells should ring and whistles blow
To celebrate the end of snow!
For winter's dark, bleak days are done.
The real new year has just begun!

Planting Seeds of Hope

Denise J. Williamson

"Conrad," Mother called as she came in from the front porch, "you got a letter from your Grandma Martin."

Conrad left his block high-rise building half-finished and ran to join Mother on the sofa in the living room. Quickly, he opened the large brown envelope and pulled out a sheet of stationery.

He began reading aloud to Mother:

Dear Conrad,

Spring is finally here. The birds are singing every morning. They make me think about gardening. I want to have a big garden again this year, even though it will be a lot of work. I hope you can come again this summer to spend a week with me. . . .

Conrad stopped. He laid the envelope and the letter on Mother's lap and began crying softly.

"What's the matter?" Mother asked gently.

Through his sniffles, Conrad explained, "I don't want to go back to the farm since Grandpa died. It won't be the same if he isn't there."

Mother and Conrad sat quietly for several minutes. Suddenly Mother said, "I think Grandma Martin sent you a present along with the letter. There's a lump in the bottom of the envelope."

Conrad reached deep and pulled out three tiny sealed white envelopes. "What's in them?" Conrad asked.

Mother looked at the labels. She read the scribbled handwriting on each packet. "Marigolds." "Zinnias." "Columbine."

"There are seeds in them," Conrad said as he held the envelopes up to the light.

"The labels are written in Grandpa Martin's handwriting," Mother said. "I'll read the rest of the letter out loud. Maybe Grandma tells why she sent them."

Mother continued the letter:

I sent you some seeds that Grandpa saved for you. He was planning to plant them with you when you came to the farm this year.

I hope you can come to help me plant the garden. But, in case you can't, I'm sending you the seeds so that you can put them in pots at your house.

Please write soon.

> *Love,*
> *Grandma*

Conrad stared at the seed packets. "Why did Grandpa have to die?" he said sadly.

"It's hard to understand, isn't it?" Mother said.

Conrad tried to finish his high-rise building, but it was no longer interesting. He put the blocks away and thought about the seeds. He decided to plant them as Grandma had asked him to do.

In the garage he found a bag of soil and some pots. The dirt smelled sweet as he filled the pots. He opened the seed packets carefully and spread the dry seeds on top of the soil. He covered them gently with a thin layer of dirt, as Grandpa Martin had taught him to do. Then, one by one, he carried the pots up to his bedroom.

"I'm glad you planted them," Mother said when Conrad showed her the potted seeds. "Now, why don't you sit down and write a letter to Grandma."

Conrad tried writing a note to tell Grandma why he couldn't come. He worked on the letter until suppertime, but still the words would not come. He was glad Mother didn't ask about it.

More than a week went by before Mother and Conrad talked about the letter again. As Mother was putting some clean socks in the drawer, Conrad came into his room to water the seeds. "Look," he exclaimed, "Grandpa's seeds are growing!" Mother was excited too.

Mother sat down on Conrad's bed and took his Bible off the nightstand. Conrad watched as she opened the book and read, "When you put a seed into the ground, it doesn't grow into a plant unless it 'dies' first. And when the green shoot comes up out of the seed, it is very different from the seed you first planted."

Conrad sat near Mother. "I didn't know the Bible talked about gardens," he said.

Mother continued, "In the same way, our earthly bodies which die are different from the bodies we shall have when we come back to life again, for they will never die."

Conrad looked at the tiny plants growing in the pots. "Those flowers are going to help me remember what you said. I'm going to tell Grandma that too." Then Conrad paused. "And," he finally said with a smile, "if it's OK with you, I'm going to tell her that I can come for a visit again this year."

Joey Tries Again   Laurel Dee Gugler

I wish Joey could do something," said Monica. "He's four years old, and he can't even walk! I learned to do a cartwheel in gymnastics yesterday. Everybody cheered."

"Monica," said Mom, "you do your best, and Joey will do his best. Your best is right for you, and Joey's best is right for him." Monica frowned and went outside to turn cartwheels. Then she went back into the house and asked, "Mom, will Joey ever turn a cartwheel?"

"He may not," answered Mom, "but he can probably learn to walk. I have an idea. Why don't you help teach him?"

"I'd rather teach him to turn a cartwheel," grumbled Monica, but she watched as Mom got Joey's favorite toy. Mom stood Joey by the couch. Then she moved one step away and held out Joey's toy. Joey reached for the toy and fell down. Mom helped him up again and held out the toy. Joey reached and fell again. "He'll never walk," complained Monica.

"He just needs lots of encouragement," said Mom.

"Well, I guess I could give him some of that."

"Sure you can," said Mom.

Monica helped Joey up and put the toy on the couch. "You can do it," she said, smiling. But Monica soon got tired. She said, "We'll have another lesson tomorrow."

She went outside, turned three cartwheels, and almost bumped into her friend, Nancy.

"Watch where you're going," said Nancy.

"Do you want to help me teach Joey to walk?" asked Monica.

"Are you kidding? He'll never learn to walk. He's stupid!"

"My brother is not stupid!" Monica exclaimed. "He has cerebral palsy, and it takes him longer to learn to walk. That doesn't make him stupid!"

"Anyway, I'm busy," said Nancy.

"We have ice cream," coaxed Monica.

The next day after school, Nancy came to Monica's house. "What kind of ice cream do you have?" asked Nancy.

"Chocolate, but we're going to teach Joey first!"

"Oh, all right. Where is he?"

Monica put Joey by the couch and held out a toy. Joey smiled and reached for it. He fell down. She helped him up again. He fell again.

"Hey, maybe he'd like my keys," said Nancy. She pulled the keys from her pocket, helped Joey up, and jingled the keys in front of him. Joey giggled, reached, and fell down. He tried to pull himself up. "He's a spunky little kid," said Nancy. Nancy and Monica helped him stand again and again.

"You can do it," said Monica.

"Come get the keys," said Nancy.

When they were tired, they had some chocolate ice cream.

Monica and Nancy played with Joey almost every day after school until . . . he could walk a few steps when he was holding onto something.

One day Mom said, "I think Joey is ready to try walking without holding on to anything."

Monica held Joey's hands and said, "Walk to Nancy." She gently let go, and Joey plopped to the floor. She tried again and again. Joey fell again and again. "We'll try again tomorrow," said Monica. "I guess he just needs more practice and encouragement."

The next day they tried again. After a while Nancy said, "I'm tired. Let's go play outside."

"Joey doesn't look tired," said Mom. "Please stay with him for a few more minutes."

"Go to Nancy," sighed Monica.

"Come to me," said Nancy. Joey took two wobbly steps and fell into Nancy's arms. Everyone cheered!

"You did it!" shouted Nancy.

"I always knew you could do it," said Monica.

Mom beamed.

Joey laughed.

"Let's celebrate with chocolate ice cream," said Monica.

Jeremy and the Jellybeans

Laurel Dee Gugler

Jeremy and his friend Skippy sat at the table with a big bag of jellybeans. (Nobody could see Skippy except Jeremy.)

Jeremy spread out all the jellybeans.

He made a long line of jellybeans.

He made jellybean designs.

He made jellybean pictures.

He made a jellybean schoolroom with rows of jellybean children and a jellybean teacher.

Then Jeremy sorted the jellybeans into piles.

He made a red pile,
  a black pile,
    a purple pile,
      a yellow pile,
        an orange pile,
          and a green pile.

The red pile was for Skippy. Skippy liked red.

The black pile was for his dad. His dad liked black ones best.

The purple pile was for his mom. She had lots of purple things.

The yellow pile was for his teacher. She had a pretty yellow dress.

The orange pile was for Jeremy. He liked the orange ones best.

The yucky green pile was for Jamie, who lived next door. Jamie had kicked him that morning.

Jeremy looked at the red pile. Skippy said, "You can have some of mine." So Jeremy did.

Jeremy looked at the black pile. He said, "Dad is not home yet. I might as well have some of his." So he did.

Jeremy looked at the purple pile. "Mom is on a diet," he said to Skippy. "I better have some of hers." So he did.

Jeremy looked at the yellow pile. Suddenly he remembered that his teacher didn't like too many sweets. "I better have some of hers too," he said. So he did.

Jeremy looked at the orange pile. "Those are for me," he said happily.

"I think I'll have some now." So he did.

Jeremy looked at the green pile. "Yuck, I hate green jellybeans," he told Skippy. "Jamie can eat those!"

Jeremy looked at the red pile again. Skippy said, "You can have one more." So Jeremy had one more red jellybean.

Jeremy looked at the black pile again. His dad still wasn't home. So Jeremy had one more black jellybean.

He looked at the purple pile and had one more purple jellybean.

He looked at the yellow pile and had one more yellow jellybean.

He looked at the orange pile and had *two* more orange jellybeans.

He looked at the green pile. "Oh yuck, Jamie can have those!" he said.

There was a knock at the door. It was Jamie.

Jeremy frowned. "If you come in, I'll make you eat these yucky green jellybeans," he said.

"I *like* green jellybeans," said Jamie, "and I'm sorry I kicked you this morning."

"That's all right. You can have the *whole* green pile," said Jeremy. "You can have some from the orange pile too." Jeremy gave Jamie some jellybeans from each pile, but. . . .
  he saved one *red* jellybean for Skippy,
    one *black* jellybean for his dad,
      one *purple* jellybean for his mom,
        and one *yellow* jellybean for his teacher.

The Beauty of the Lily   Frances Jenkins Olcott

Once upon a time, in a far-distant land, there dwelt a peasant named Ivan, and with him lived his little nephew Vasily.

Ivan was gloomy and unkempt, and his restless eyes looked out from his matted hair and beard. As for the little Vasily, he was a manly child; but though his uncle was kind enough to him in his way, he neither washed him, nor combed his hair, nor taught him anything.

The hut they lived in was very miserable. Its walls were full of holes, the furniture of its one room was broken down and dusty, and its floor unswept. The little garden was filled with stones and weeds. The neighbors passing by in the daytime turned aside their heads. But they never passed at night, for fear of Ivan.

Now it happened one Easter morning that Ivan, feeling restless, rose early and went and stood before the door of the hut. The trees were budding, the air was full of bird songs, the dew lay glittering on the grass, and a nearby brook ran leaping and gurgling along. The rays of the rising sun shone slanting from the tops of the distant hills and seemed to touch the hut.

And as Ivan looked, he saw a young man coming swiftly and lightly from the hills, and he bore on his arm a sheaf of pure white lilies. The stranger drew near, and stopped before the hut.

"Christ is risen!" he said in flutelike tones.

"He is risen indeed!" muttered Ivan through his beard.

Then the young man took a lily from his sheaf and gave it to Ivan, saying, "Keep it white!" And, smiling, he passed on.

Wonderingly Ivan gazed at the flower in his hand. Its gold-green stem seemed to support a pure white crown—or was it a translucent cup filled with light! And as the man looked into the flower's gold-fringed heart, awe stole into his soul.

Then he turned and entered the hut, saying to himself, "I will put it in water."

But when he went to lay the lily on the window sill, so that he might search for a vessel to set it in, he dared not put it down, for the sill was covered with thick dust.

He turned to the table, but its top was soiled with crumbs of moldy bread and cheese mingled with dirt. He looked about the room, and not one spot could he see where he might lay the lily without sullying its pure loveliness.

He called the little Vasily, and bade him stand and hold the flower. He then searched for something to put it in. He found an empty bottle which he carried to the brook and washed and filled with sparkling water. This he placed upon the table, and in it set the lily.

Then as he looked at the begrimed hands of little Vasily he thought to himself, *When I leave the room, he may touch the flower and soil it.* So he took the child and washed him, and combed his yellow hair; and the little one seemed to bloom like the lily itself. And Ivan gazed on him in amazement, murmuring, "I never saw him thus before!"

From that hour a change came over Ivan. He cared tenderly for the little Vasily. He washed himself and combed his own hair. He cleaned the hut and mended its walls and furniture. He carried away the weeds and stones from the garden. He sowed flowers and planted vegetables. And the neighbors passing by no longer turned their heads aside, but stopping, talked with Ivan, and sometimes gave the little Vasily presents of clothes and toys.

As for the lily, seven days it blossomed in freshness and beauty, and gave forth a delicate fragrance; but on the eighth day, when Ivan and Vasily woke, it was gone. And though they sought it in hut and garden, they did not find it.

So Ivan and the little Vasily worked from day to day among their flowers and vegetables, and talked to their neighbors, and were happy. When the long winter nights came, Ivan read aloud about the lilies of the field, that toil not, neither do they spin, yet Solomon in all his glory was not arrayed like them. He read of the beloved that feedeth among the lilies, and of the Rose of Sharon and the lily-of-the-valley.

So Easter came again. And early, very early in the morning, Ivan and the little Vasily arose and dressed, and went and stood before the hut. And when the splendor of the coming day shone above the distant hills, lo! the young man came swiftly and lightly, and in his arms he bore crimson roses.

He drew near, and, stopping before the hut, said sweetly, "Christ is risen!"

"He is risen, indeed!" responded Ivan and Vasily joyously.

"How beautiful is thy lily!" said the young man.

"Alas!" answered Ivan, "it is vanished away, and we know not whither."

"Its beauty lives in thy heart," said the young man. "It can never die!"

And he took from his arm a crimson rose and gave it to Vasily, saying, "Keep it fresh!"

But he smiled tenderly at Ivan, and passed on.

I'm a Garden Helper

Shirley Pope Waite

Spade and shovel, rake and hoe.
Tools that help a garden grow.

First I help my daddy spade.
See the hole that I have made?

Then I rake to break each clod,
To help my daddy smooth the sod.

After we have planted seeds,
We'll try to keep out all the weeds.

That's when I'll use my little hoe,
To give the plants a chance to grow.

God does the rest when we are done,
With gentle rain, and warm, bright sun.

Puddles

Donna Lugg Pape

It's rain that makes the puddles,
And God who makes the rain.
Oh, I love puddles anywhere.
I love a puddly lane.

Puddles are a lot of fun,
And on a sunny day
It's fun to look and see myself
In happy puddle play.

I'm glad God helps make puddles;
For most of all, I think,
A puddle is especially nice
So birds can take a drink.

Not Big Enough
Martha Tolles

*E*ddy and his little sister, Penny, hurried through the park gates to join the crowd of children for the Easter egg hunt.

"Now you stay close to me, Penny," Eddy warned her. "Pick up as many eggs as you can, and if you see a golden one, be sure to take that one. Then you win the prize."

Just then a whistle was blown, and someone cut the string.

"Hooray!" the children shouted and scrambled forward to look for eggs. Right away Eddy spied a red egg behind a bush, then a purple one in the tall grass, then a green one. Soon he was jumping from place to place excitedly gathering the eggs and dropping them into his basket.

"Come on, Penny," he shouted over his shoulder.

Finally Eddy paused to count his eggs, and when he looked around for Penny she was gone.

"Penny, Penny," he called frantically, but there was no sign of Penny's little blond pony tail and pink dress. Eddy ran one way and another looking for her.

"Penny," he called sadly but it was useless.

Eddy carefully set his basketful of eggs down on the grass and walked idly over to some boxes. He kicked at a couple and then peered into a big one that was standing on end. There lying curled up in the box was Penny, hair all mussed, face flushed, and new pink dress crumpled all around her. She was fast asleep!

Now that he had found her, Eddy began to feel cross. "You're just not big enough to go to egg hunts," he said.

Eddy started to pull Penny to her feet so they could look for the golden egg again. Suddenly he heard a piercing whistle. It was too late. The Easter egg hunt had ended.

"Oh, Eddy," Penny squealed, wide awake now and suddenly jumping to her feet. "I found something for you." She let go of her wrinkled skirt and out rolled the golden egg onto the ground. "It's for you Eddy, because you brought me to the egg hunt." The egg glistened in the sunshine.

Eddy stood still, too surprised to move for a minute. Then he scooped up the egg and ran, waving it in the air. Penny followed at his heels.

"Wait, look, we have it!" Eddy shouted joyfully. "Look, my sister found it." The egg gleamed brightly as Eddy handed it up to Jerry, the judge.

Jerry's red faced beamed as he took the egg from Eddy and handed him a soft little bunny. "Where did you find it, Penny?" Jerry asked her as she came puffing up beside Eddy.

"It was near those boxes," Penny explained. "After I found it, I thought I would just wait there for Eddy."

"Here, Penny," Eddy said, turning to her with the bunny cupped in his hands. "The bunny is really yours."

"Oh, no," Penny said, drawing back a little. She patted the bunny very cautiously. "I gave the egg to you, Eddy. Besides, I don't want the bunny. I'm not big enough."

The Thirdhand Bike

Lucille Ellison

Lucy thought her "new" thirdhand bike was super. It looked so smooth and shiny sitting there in the machinery shed. It had been her two older brothers', and now with fresh paint and a "tune-up" it would be hers. She could hardly wait to ride it to school.

Breakfast on Monday morning seemed to take longer than usual. Lucy didn't even mind the "yucky" tasting oatmeal. Grabbing her schoolbag, she waved good-bye to Mom, and took off on her bike down the country road on her way to the school, a half mile away. She felt as if she were flying free as a bird. The wind blew cool air on her face. It felt good.

Before long she was at the driveway to Murray's farm.

"New bike, huh?" Murray asked indifferently.

"No, not really. It was my brothers' bike. We painted it, and now it's mine," Lucy explained.

"I'll bet you wish you really had a new one," Murray said, glancing at his own new bike.

Lucy could see that Murray didn't think too much of her bike. But it really didn't matter what he thought, she decided. She'd show him that her bike was OK. What more could she want? Blue sky overhead, huge old maples along the road, and flying wheels beneath her.

At school, the morning crept by. Lucy's teacher, Mrs. Riddells, was crosser than usual, but Lucy didn't care. In her mind, she was sailing down the big hill near the Shantz farm, enjoying the trees, fields, and fences as they flashed by.

Dong, dong the old school bell rang, signaling the end of the morning. Lucy was going home for lunch today. With this bike, she could make better time than ever before. Besides, now she didn't have to pedal as fast as on her old one-speed bike. Lucy, Murray, and another friend, Janet, all started home together. Janet turned off at her road. Then it happened! Murray, with a snickering laugh, wove in and out in front of Lucy's bike. She swerved quickly and fell to the hard pavement.

Crash! Her leg stung. It was bleeding. Even though her leg hurt badly, Lucy was not going to cry.

"Heh, heh! How come the new bike crashed, eh?" Murray asked carelessly. Off he rode into his driveway.

For Lucy, the rest of the ride home seemed like a mile. Her leg throbbed with pain! Tears of anger ran down her face. At last she saw her mother in the yard. Bursting into tears she told the whole story.

"I hate him, I hate him, Mom," she cried. "I'm not going back to school this afternoon." Carefully, Mother washed the scraped leg and put some Band-Aids on it. After that it felt a lot better. Still there was a heavy, angry feeling inside of Lucy. How she hated Murray! Why would anyone try to make her fall on purpose?

Before she knew it, it was time to go back to school for the afternoon. Lucy hoped that Murray had already left. Then she wouldn't have to ride with him. No such luck! There he was, waiting at the end of his driveway.

Eyeing her bandaged leg, he said quietly, "Lucy, about that fall—I guess I was to blame. I'm sorry."

"It's OK," Lucy replied. "I'm not very steady with this bike yet. Give me a couple of days and I just might be a champion biker." They both laughed.

Way down deep, Lucy knew that the heavy, angry feeling had disappeared. Once again she felt like she was flying along on her thirdhand bike.

In All Things Beautiful Carol Ryrie Brink

*T*herese and Grand'mere were going to church in the great cathedral of Notre Dame in Paris. They had traveled many miles from their little home village to hear the Easter service. Grand'mere had told Therese how beautiful it would be. But it was even more beautiful than Therese had imagined.

All in their best black dresses, they came through the sunny spring morning to the open square where the great church stood. Then Therese clutched Grand'mere's hand tightly and looked a long time, for she had never seen so large a church nor one so old. Above the three great doors were statues of the saints, and the two great towers seemed almost to touch the clouds.

Inside the cathedral it was cool and dark except where the sunshine came through the stained-glass windows in rays of red and blue and yellow and purple. The stone pillars went up and up, and finally branched like trees far, far above their heads. But most beautiful of all was the big rose window which shone with a thousand lovely colors. Side by side Grand'mere and Therese knelt to pray and to take part in the Easter service. Therese's knees grew stiff from kneeling so long in the chilly air, but she was very happy. The cathedral had been decorated with flowers and lighted candles, and everywhere was sweetness and beauty. Then came the most wonderful thing of all—better even than the great rose window! A beautiful music began to fill the great church. Therese clutched Grand'mere's sleeve.

"Grand'mere," she whispered, "is it God's voice?"

"Hush, my little one," answered Grand'mere. "It is only the great organ of which I have told you." Therese clasped her hands and listened. The deep notes seemed to make the whole church tremble. The high notes were like the singing of birds. Then many happy voices joined the music of the organ. Therese had never heard anything so lovely.

At last the service was over and the people began to leave. Therese and Grand'mere stayed a long time, looking at the beautiful church. When they could stay no longer they dropped money in the box for the poor beside the great door and went outside. The square in front of the great church seemed very bright and warm. Therese turned for another look at the great doors and high towers which had been built so long ago.

"Are you not hungry, my rabbit?" said Grand'mere. "Let us cross the river and get lunch before we start for home."

"Oh, Grand'mere, how sparkling the river is! How nice the sunshine feels! Tell me truly, Grand'mere, was that not God's voice we heard in the church?"

Grand'mere's black eyes were very bright in her brown, wrinkled face. She smiled and nodded her head softly, so that her little white cap string bobbed up and down in the spring breeze. "God's voice is in everything beautiful, my little one," she said wisely.

As they crossed the river they heard a great singing and twittering of birds.

"Listen, Grand'mere!" cried Therese. "It sounds like the country, only sweeter. Oh, listen!" In an open square beside the river was the flower and bird market. Little stalls about the edge of the square were full of gaily colored flowers, and in the center were hundreds of cages of birds. Each merchant had his cages set out on a table before him. There were parrots and love birds, pigeons and cockatoos. But dearest of all were the canaries. They almost burst their little throats singing springtime gladness. Therese went among them, walking softly so as not to frighten them. Her heart was so happy she wanted to sing, too. Lunch was forgotten as she and Grand'mere went from cage to cage, listening and admiring.

"Come, *petite*," said Grand'mere at last. "Surely we have seen them all."

"But no! Here is one more," cried Therese. Sure enough, there was one more cage. A little boy in a ragged black apron was holding it upon his knees, and it was the yellowest and happiest canary of all.

"Where are the rest of your birds?" asked Therese.

"I have only one," answered the boy.

"You have only one, and you wish to sell it?" cried Therese, surprised. "But why?"

"It is because my mother is sick and we must have money to buy her medicine. Besides, we can no longer feed the little bird, because we must have all the crumbs for ourselves."

"Oh, Grand'mere," cried Therese, "is it not sad?" Grand'mere's wrinkled fingers began to fumble in her black purse. The canary looked at Therese with his bright black eyes. Then he swelled out his yellow throat and began to sing. Therese closed her eyes and clasped her hands. His song made her remember the high, trembling notes of the organ. Grand'mere was looking at the price marked on the cage. It was almost as many francs as she had in her purse. She couldn't quite decide what to do.

"Therese," said Grand'mere. "I have some bread in my bag, left from our breakfast. Will that do for our lunch?"

"Oh, yes, Grand'mere," cried Therese, guessing what Grand'mere meant. "Oh, please do let us buy the bird from the poor boy."

Grand'mere counted the money into the boy's eager palm. When it was all counted, she slipped in an extra franc for himself. Then Therese took the little cage in her own hands. Now the bird belonged to Grand'mere and her!

"Oh, Grand'mere," said Therese, "think how wonderful it will be to hear it sing every day—not just this once, but every day."

Grand'mere nodded her head and smiled wisely. "When the little bird sings, Therese," said Grand'mere, "we must listen well, for we shall hear it sing of happiness and beauty. It is one way God tells us of them."

Lilies for Someone Special

Frances Carfi Matranga

*I*t was the day before Easter, and Susan was counting the money she and Skippy had saved up together. Susan was ten and good at figures. Skippy was only six.

"Five dollars and fifty cents!" she announced proudly. "That ought to be enough to buy a nice lily plant. We'll get it at the supermarket. They cost less there than at the nursery. But I want a real nice one."

Skippy nodded gravely. "Real nice one," he repeated.

Susan liked the way Skippy listened to her when she spoke, as though what she had to say was important. She knew it was because of the way she treated him. She never slapped him the way some girls with little brothers did. Nor did she yell at him when he did something wrong. Well, almost never. She had found it pays to be nice to little kids and explain things to them, because then they behave better. Not like that Marian next door. She was mean to her little brother, and he did everything he could to torment her. It served her right. Little kids were people too, after all.

Susan had explained to Skippy whom the Easter plant was for, and why, and he was almost as excited about it as she was.

"We'll go right after lunch and pick out the best one we can find," she told him. "They still have quite a few plants at Grand Union. Mom is going to drive us there."

They were so eager to be off that they could hardly sit still at the table.

"Finish your milk, Skippy," Mother said. "Don't worry. They won't sell out before we get there."

"Our Easter plant is for somebody special," Skippy said.

Mother smiled.

"It's not for you, Mom," Susan said quickly, lest their mother misunderstand. "Not that you aren't special. But we have only enough money for one present, and it took weeks to save it up."

"Took weeks to save it up," Skippy echoed.

"Is it for Daddy?" Mother asked.

"Of course not," Susan said. "Do you think we'd give Daddy a present, and none for you? In that case, the lily would be for both of you."

Mother looked puzzled. "So who is it for?"

The children exchanged glances and giggled.

"Let's tell her," Skippy said, clapping his hands.

"Not yet." Susan's eyes were twinkling. "Help us pick out a nice plant, Mom, and then the three of us can give it together. Right after we buy it."

"Well, I must say I'm curious," Mother admitted. "When my children do without their allowance for several weeks, it must be for somebody very special indeed. Skippy, Dad's fixing something in the basement. Run down and tell him we're taking the car to go to the store."

A little later, at the supermarket, they examined the lily plants and selected one with four lovely white blooms and two in bud. It cost $5.98 plus tax. The children didn't have quite enough money, so Mother put in the extra change needed. The plant pot had green foil around it and a white ribbon tied in a big bow.

"Pretty," Susan said with a happy smile.

"Where do we go from here?" Mother wanted to know as they got into the car.

"I'll direct you," Susan said, holding the potted plant on her lap.

"No, let me do it," begged Skippy,

who was sitting between them. "You go that-a-way, Mom," he said, jerking his thumb to the right.

"Aha!" Mother said, smiling. "I bet we're taking the plant to someone in the hospital. Anybody I know?"

"Yes, Mom, it's for someone you know," Susan told her, the twinkle in her eye again.

"Someone you know," Skippy said, nodding happily. "Now turn this way."

Five minutes later, they were at their church. Since Mother was the organist, she had her own key. She smiled as they went inside. They walked up the aisle, and Susan placed the lily on the altar.

The three of them knelt, and Susan said, "The flowers are for you, Jesus. For you, not just to decorate the church. Thank you for being our Savior, and rising again from the dead. Without you there would be no joy and no life everlasting. I love you."

"Happy Easter, Jesus!" Skippy's voice rang out in the church.

Mother's eyes were moist. "Hallelujah," she said softly.

I Am Trusting You, Lord Jesus

Frances R. Havergal

I am trusting you, Lord Jesus,
Trusting only you;
Trusting you for full salvation,
Free and true.

I am trusting you for pardon;
At your feet I bow,
For your grace and tender mercy
Trusting now.

I am trusting you to guide me;
You alone shall lead,
Ev'ry day and hour supplying
All my need.

I am trusting you, Lord Jesus;
Never let me fall.
I am trusting you forever
And for all.

Phantom Eggs

Brigid Casey-Meyer

Beth walked into her grandmother's living room and stopped short, staring at dozens of brightly decorated Easter eggs. "Gram!" she gasped. "I never knew you had so many!"

"Yes, I do have a lot," Gram said, looking around. "I'm glad you came, dear. You can help me sort through them. I told the children's librarians that this year they could have the display earlier."

Beth knelt in front of the sofa where several eggs were lying. "Didn't the Phantom give it to you?" She carefully held up a sequin-encrusted egg.

"Yes, and it's one of my favorites. I got it about ten years ago. I've decided to make a special display this year of eggs from the Phantom—in his memory."

Beth stared at her grandmother. "What do you mean 'in his memory?' Was Gramps the Phantom?"

"Yes, Beth, it was Gramps. Every Easter morning from the time we were married I found a tiny basket with a handmade Easter egg in it on the doorstep." Gram's smile started to waver a little. "Every egg was different. Easter just won't seem the same this year without the Phantom. That's why I decided to let the library have the display early. There won't be a new egg to wait for this year."

Beth got up to hug her grandmother. "Did Gramps know that you knew that he was the Phantom?" she asked.

Gram wiped her eyes on the corner of the apron she was wearing. "Oh, I'm sure he suspected I knew that it was him, but I never let on. It was kind of a delightful game that we played with each other. Every year before Easter he'd spend hours in his workshop and never tell me what he was doing. I'm sure he practiced on a lot of eggs. You know what a perfectionist he was." Gram laughed through misty eyes. "I'd give a lot to know what he did with all those eggs!"

Beth laughed too. "Did Gramps fix breakfast a lot?"

"Now that I think of it, he did. And I'll bet you can guess what we usually had."

"Eggs!" Beth shouted.

The rest of the afternoon passed pleasantly as they sorted and packed the eggs. Gram had a story to tell about each one.

That evening at supper Beth was quiet.

"Is anything wrong, Beth?" her mother asked.

"How far away is Easter?"

"About four weeks," her mother replied. "Why?"

"I'm going to make an Easter egg," Beth said slowly.

"We always color eggs, Beth," her mother said, puzzled. "Don't you think this is a bit early to start?"

"No, because I want to make a fancy egg—like Gram has in her collection."

A look of understanding spread across Mother's face. "Were you helping Gram get her eggs ready for the library display this week?"

Beth nodded. "And do you know what? I found out that Gramps was the Phantom all along. Did you know that, Mom?"

"Did I ever! I remember all the eggs we used to eat. It's a wonder I didn't sprout feathers when I was growing up!" Mother smiled at the memory. "I never let on to Gramps that I knew though. It would have spoiled his fun. He got such a kick out of surprising Gram."

"She's really sad because this is going to be the first Easter in almost 50 years that she won't be getting a Phantom egg," Beth said. "I thought that if I could make her one, she might feel a little better. I know it wouldn't be the same as one from the Phantom, but I'd like to try."

Beth's father, who had been listening quietly, smiled at his daughter. "I think that's a great idea, Beth. It would remind Gram that she is still loved even though Gramps isn't here anymore. If I can do anything to help, let me know."

After school the next day Beth bicycled over to the library. She found several books to take home on the art of egg decorating. When she finished her homework and the dishes, she sat down to study the books before bedtime. As Mother gave her a kiss good night, Beth said, "Mom, some of those eggs that Gramps made took a lot of time and work. Why didn't he make some to sell?"

"He only made them for Gram because he loved her, and he knew how much she liked decorated eggs. Have you decided what kind you're going to make?"

"Not yet. But I've got the choice narrowed down. I'll decide in the morning." Beth yawned and snuggled down under the covers.

By Saturday Beth was eager to start her project. She had decided to try her hand at two different types of decorations. One involved an onion-skin dye. After the egg had been dyed, a design would be scratched onto its surface. The other type was a "sugar" egg. This required some diamond dust and floral cake decorations as well as glue, ribbons, and a special sugar frosting. Both types required starting with clean, whole, empty eggshells.

A few hours later Beth looked ruefully into a bowl of shell-less eggs. The yellow yolks seemed to be winking at her. She had only a few whole shells to show for her efforts.

She looked up when Mother came into the kitchen. "Mom, can I fix breakfast this morning?"

Mother put an arm around Beth's shoulders and hugged her sympathetically. "Don't worry, honey. We'll be happy to eat all the eggs we need to. If I never clucked before, I doubt that I will now."

"Thanks, Mom. You're super. This isn't as easy as I thought."

The weeks sped by. Beth practiced her egg craft every spare moment. The family ate omelets, angel food cake, souffles, custards, meringue pies, and anything else they could think of that used lots of eggs. Decorated eggshells lined every available space.

The day before Easter came quickly. Beth's mother had rummaged through the attic and found a beautiful little basket that was the perfect size for one egg. Beth had lined it with soft Easter grass.

After supper Beth carefully positioned her prize egg in the basket. Pastel flowers shone softly through its glistening spun-sugar coating.

"Beth, that's lovely," her mother said.

"You've done a great job, honey," her father agreed. "You should be proud of yourself. We are. I'm sure Gram will be very happy."

"Thank you." Beth smiled. "It did turn out nice, didn't it? I'm glad I decided to do this kind instead of the onion-skin type. I like this kind better."

"I like the smell better too." Her dad wrinkled his nose in mock disgust at the remembered smell of boiling onion skins.

"Oh, Dad!" Beth laughed. "I can't wait to see Gram's face."

Early the next morning they drove to Gram's house and parked out of sight down the street. Beth cautiously crept up to the front door, put the basket on the steps, rang the bell, and scurried behind a huge lilac bush.

The front door opened slowly. Beth's grandmother stepped out and peered around uncertainly. Shaking her head, she turned to go back inside. Suddenly she glanced down and froze as if she couldn't believe her eyes.

Beth held her breath as Gram sat down on the step and placed the basket on her lap. She stared and stared at it. Beth could see tears on her grandmother's cheeks. Gram lifted her head and called out, "If you're out there, my new Phantom, how can I thank you? You've made me very happy. I'm going to call my granddaughter to tell her about your kindness. She'll be delighted."

As soon as Gram closed the door, Beth scooted back to the car. "Quick!" she told her parents. "We've got to get home. Gram is going to call me to tell me about the egg."

The phone was ringing as Beth raced through the front door. Although Beth was winded from her run, her grandmother was too excited to notice it over the phone.

Easter dinner conversation revolved around the new Phantom egg which Gram had brought to show off. All the aunts, uncles, and cousins were impressed, and Beth glowed inwardly when Gram said, "Tomorrow I'm taking this egg right down to the library and have it put in the case with my other Phantom eggs. I'm going to make a nice card explaining what happened and how much this egg means to me. Somehow I'm sure that Gramps is pleased too."

Big Shot

Martha Tolles

Robbie bent over his handle bars. He was in a hurry to sign up for a paper route so he would be the most important kid on the block.

Up ahead he saw an older boy, Michael, walking along the sidewalk. And as he passed him, Michael looked up and waved. "Hi, Robbie," he called out. Robbie waved back, pleased to be noticed by an older boy. He had heard that Michael was hoping for a paper route, too.

As he whizzed off down the street, he thought, Michael doesn't even have a bike. How can he ever get a route?

There was a line of boys and girls at Mr. Hansen's house. Mr. Hansen was busy taking down their names. Robbie wondered how many jobs were open for delivering the *Evening Standard*. Jack and Jennifer had both had routes before. They were sure to get jobs.

When Mr. Hansen got through with everybody, he said, "I'll let you know in a few days. I need three people for the routes this spring. Thanks for coming."

Robbie felt discouraged as he rode home. Jack and Jennifer were sure to get routes. That left just one more. *What chance do I have?* he thought.

Robbie tried to forget about the paper route the next day. It was another sunny spring day, and he played soccer at the playground until late.

On the way home he noticed dark clouds piling up in the sky. Soon it began to rain. Thunder rumbled in the distance. Robbie shivered and rode faster.

Then, just as he came to Mr. Hansen's house, he noticed the evening paper lying out near the curb. *I ought to put Mr. Hansen's paper on the porch for him*, he thought. He jumped off his bike, grabbed the paper, and started for the house. Just then Mr. Hansen came out on his porch.

"Hi, Mr. Hansen." Robbie hurried toward him.

"That's nice of you. Say, weren't you here yesterday?"

Robbie nodded, pleased that Mr. Hansen remembered him. "Yes, I was."

Mr. Hansen looked off into the rain. "I've been thinking about the routes," he said. "I'm giving one to Jack and one to Jennifer. They did a good job before." Robbie held his breath. "I could give the other one to you." Robbie's hopes rose. "Or I could give it to Michael."

"Michael doesn't have a bike," Robbie said before he could stop himself.

"I know," Mr. Hansen nodded. "He's offered to walk the route. That way he could earn money for one."

Robbie glanced through the rain toward his gleaming red racing bike. He had received it as a Christmas gift. Robbie knew what he should do. It would be fun to have a route now, of course. He could see himself flying down the street on his bike, tossing papers on all the lawns, and all the little kids admiring him.

"Let Michael have the route." He looked up at Mr. Hansen. "I'm younger anyway."

Mr. Hansen smiled down at him. "I tell you what then. The next route that comes along is yours."

Robbie grinned. "Okay, thanks, Mr. Hansen." It was nice to know that he would have a paper route later, and in the meantime Michael could get his bike.

As Robbie ran through the rain toward his bike, he had the strangest feeling. Somehow, he felt important already.

Receiving the Light
Phyllis S. Yingling

My mother got to go with Dad on a business trip to New York City, and I got to spend four days with Elena and her family. It was a busy time for them because it was their Greek Orthodox Easter celebration. Mom told me to be sure to behave.

When I came over on Thursday afternoon, the Pappas family was getting ready to dye hard-boiled eggs. Elena's dad, as the head of the household, dipped the first egg into the dark red dye. Grandmother Pappas said the red color represents the blood of Jesus. When Elena's mother agreed to let us dye some of the eggs in other colors, I could tell that Grandmother Pappas wasn't happy about breaking the tradition of having all red eggs. I wondered what we were going to do with all the eggs. We must have dyed about six dozen of them. Elena and I were colored from head to toe.

Grandmother Pappas used some of the eggs to decorate the special Easter bread she made. Just before each loaf was baked, she tucked a dyed egg into the dough so that the egg showed when the loaf came out of the oven.

On Friday evening I went to the church service with the family. At the end, all the people followed the priests out into the street, carrying candles. The line wound around the block and back again to the church. I had my own candle, and I watched very carefully to keep it from blowing out.

Saturday was a day of preparation. Elena and I spent the afternoon cleaning up her room and helping her mother prepare for the Easter feast.

At eleven o'clock that night we all went to the church. Soon the huge church was filled to overflowing. The crowd grew quiet as a chanter sang hymns from the choir loft. At exactly midnight, the lights of the church went out. It was as dark as can be. I was a little bit scared. Then from behind the screen in front of the altar, the priest appeared, holding a lighted candle. *"Defte lavete fos* (DEL-te LA-ve-te fos)," he said. "Receive the Light." He lit the candle of the assistant priest, who then lit the candles of ten altar boys. They went through the church lighting the candles of one person in each pew. As the light was passed from person to person, the darkness went away and the church was glowing with light.

After the service we all went to the church social hall for refreshments. There was cheese and fruit and olives and red Easter eggs, and red wine for the grown-ups. It was a happy time. People were calling *Christos anesti* (kree-STOS ah-NEH-stee)—Christ is risen—to each other and answering *Alethos anesti* (Ah-lee-THOS ah-NEH-stee)—Truly He is risen.

We all had fun trying to see who had the strongest eggs. Elena said, "Let me see your egg." I held the red egg up, and she knocked her egg against mine and cracked it. "Aha!" she laughed, "now you try." I picked another egg from a plate on the table, held it tight and knocked her egg as hard as I could. My egg cracked! "Ha!" she cried, "I've got a champion egg." She went around to her family cracking everybody's eggs with her "lucky" egg until finally her cousin Tony cracked it with his egg. I had been sleepy in church, but now I was wide awake. It's a good thing, too, because there was more to come.

When we went home there was a feast waiting for us. We had roast lamb, a delicious soup called *mageretsa* (ma-yeh-REE-tsah), more red eggs, and of course the Easter bread. As we ate, Mr. Pappas asked his mother how she liked the service at church. Do you know, this is the first year she had ever attended. It used to be that only men attended the Easter service. The women stayed home and prepared the meal—and waited for the men to return. She had done that all these years. Now her face lit up as she thought about the service.

It was nearly four o'clock in the morning when we got to bed, so I slept until noon. When I came downstairs, I saw my parents were home. Elena and I gathered up some more eggs and took them to my mom and dad. I had so much to tell them! My parents wanted to go back over to the Pappas' house to thank them for keeping me. Would you believe it? We all ate some more red Easter eggs. Now I knew why we'd dyed so many. I patted my stomach. I thought if I ate one more egg I'd begin to cluck! It had been a wonderful celebration of Easter—one I would never forget.

Spring Noises

Jacqueline Rowland

What sound does spring make, as it starts to come?
Does it shout or whistle or buzz or hum?
Does it tweet or rustle or screech or blare,
When springtime signs are everywhere?

What sound does a yellow butterfly make?
Can you hear its chrysalis rattle and break?
A small brown seed, can you hear it shout
As it splits its sides and starts to sprout?
And bears and groundhogs, the animal crowd,
When winter's over, do they yawn out loud?

I love spring noises, loud and small—
But I like its whispers the best of all!

The Best Present

Wendy Pfeffer

*I*t was spring. And for Charlie, spring was absolutely the best time of year, because what Charlie loved to do most in the whole world was to go for long walks to all his favorite places.

Today he had even more reason for wanting to take one of his long walks. It was his mother's birthday, and he didn't have a present. He didn't want just any present. He wanted to give his mom the best present in the whole world. So he set out to find it.

He walked by Mr. Hobson's rose garden, stopped, and took a deep breath. *Mmmm,* here was the best smell in the whole world. But he couldn't pick Mr. Hobson's prize roses for mom's birthday. He had once, and got spanked.

So he walked on.

Soon he came to his favorite sitting place, an old crooked stump with soft green moss covering it. Charlie sat down. "Nice, but too heavy to carry home for Mom," he mumbled.

So he walked on.

Farther on Charlie stopped to taste the icy cold water in the brook, the best taste in the whole world. But Charlie knew by the time he'd scooped it up and carried it home, it wouldn't be icy cold anymore.

So he walked on.

A little later, sitting quietly in the grass, Charlie heard sweet music. He watched a grasshopper run his wings together to make the sweet music—the best music. What a great present for mom! Charlie reached out to take the grasshopper home. But, the grasshopper spat brown juice, leaped into the air and disappeared.

So Charlie walked on.

Nearby, there was a rotting log, the best place to find spotted salamanders, so small and soft and pretty—a great pet for mom. Charlie squatted and took a tiny salamander in his hands. It wriggled and wriggled. Charlie watched it squirm. Was it frightened? Unhappy? Charlie let it go. It belonged in the rotting log.

So Charlie walked on.

Finally, he found something perfect, the best present in the whole world, a lacy spider web sparkling with dew drops. It even held the spider, still spinning. Carefully, Charlie pulled one end of the web, then the other. The spider hurried away as the web became a bundle of sticky threads in Charlie's hands. Charlie wiped his hands on his pants, turned around and headed home.

He'd seen all the best things in the whole world and he still didn't have a present for his mom. Suddenly, he knew what he'd give her.

He raced home, and called out, "Come with me, Mom."

And she did.

She smelled the best smell in the whole world in Mr. Hobson's garden.

Charlie showed her the old crooked stump, and they sat together on the best sitting place in the whole world.

Mom tasted the best water in the whole world, right out of Charlie's scooped hands.

She listened to the grasshopper play the best music.

Mom peeked under the best salamander finding place and saw a tiny yellow spotted salamander.

Then, she watched the best web spinner in the whole world spin a brand new sparkling web.

"Happy Birthday," Charlie said.

"Thank you, Charlie," said his mother, placing a kiss on the middle of his forehead. "That was the best present in the whole world."

"The best present for the best mom," said Charlie.

All Things Bright and Beautiful

Gay Bell

Erin tapped on the goldfish bowl, but Jeremiah didn't move. Jeremiah lay on his side at the bottom of the bowl. Erin could see his gills go in and out very slowly. She sprinkled some fish food in the bowl, but Jeremiah still didn't move.

"Something's wrong with Jeremiah!" Erin hollered.

Erin's daddy looked at Jeremiah. "The fish is sick, Erin. I think he is going to die."

"No!" said Erin. "I won't let Jeremiah die!" Her eyes filled with tears. "No!" Erin stamped her foot. She ran to her mother. "Mommy! Jeremiah's sick. Daddy says he's going to die. Do something, Mommy. Please!"

Mommy put her arm around Erin. "I'm sorry, Erin, but I can't do anything."

Erin felt a scared feeling settle over her. She started to sob. Mommy picked up Erin and sat in the rocking chair.

"I tried to take good care of Jeremiah," said Erin.

"I think you did take good care of him," Mommy said. "But sometimes, no matter how much we love something, and no matter how much good care we give it, it dies."

"Like Grandpa?" Erin looked up at her mother's face.

"Like Grandpa," Mommy kept on rocking her. "Grandfather was very sick. Daddy and I did everything we could to try to make him well. The doctor did everything she could to make him well."

"But Grandpa died," said Erin.

"Yes, he died," said Mommy.

For a long time, Erin didn't say anything. She listened to the creak, creak of the chair. She snuggled close to Mommy.

Finally, she slid from Mommy's lap and walked over to the fishbowl. Jeremiah was floating upside down on the water.

"Jeremiah died," Erin said to her mother. "Do you think Jeremiah will go to heaven, like Grandpa?"

"That's a hard question to answer," said Mommy. "I don't know if anyone knows for sure." She put her arm around Erin. "One thing I do know for sure—God loves us very much, and even though we don't understand exactly how it happens, God has promised that when we die God will give us new life. We will have a happy new life with God."

"Jeremiah too?"

Mommy nodded. "I think maybe that includes Jeremiah."

Erin climbed back on Mommy's lap.

"Do you remember the song Miss Joy taught you at church school?" Mommy began to sing the words softly:

> "All things bright and beautiful,
>   All creatures great and small,
> All things wise and wonderful:
>   The Lord God made them all."

After a few minutes, Erin sang too.

Apple Blossom Ride
Helen Mallmann

I wish my class didn't have to go to Garfield School on Monday," grumbled Tommy. He was riding with his dad to the apple orchard.

"Why don't you want to go?" his dad asked.

"The special ed kids go to Garfield School," answered Tommy. "I don't know any of them. I'd rather go to the nature center at the state park."

"Maybe when you talk to one of the Garfield kids, you won't feel so uncomfortable," his dad said.

"I don't know what to say," said Tommy.

"You could ask him if he's been to an apple orchard," said his dad. "If he hasn't, you could tell him about it."

"We're going to do some stuff with the kids," said Tommy. "What if he can't do it?"

"If he needs help, help him."

"I think I'll get sick Monday," said Tommy.

They passed blossoming trees, white against the blue May sky. Dad slowed the car and turned into the driveway.

In the big barn a teenage boy told them that the trailer was out in the orchard, taking people on a tour. While they waited for it to return, he showed Tommy and his dad the barn.

The teenager opened the large walk-in cooler door. The smell of apples and the cold temperature met them as they stepped inside. Wooden boxes were stacked at one end of the room. Inside them were the apples left over from the fall crop.

Tommy and his dad looked at the grading machine that sorted the apples by size.

In the store Tommy's dad bought him a caramel apple on a stick. He slurped apple juice as they waited outside on a bench in the warm sunshine.

"Tommy, who made those apple trees?" asked his dad, pointing to the orchard.

"God did," answered Tommy.

"Right," said Dad. "Are they all alike?"

"All of them have blossoms and leaves," said Tommy, wondering why his dad was asking him that. "And they all have a trunk and branches and roots."

"Yes," said his dad. "Are children alike, too?"

"We all have to breathe and eat and sleep," said Tommy, "and all of us have feelings. We talked about it in health class."

"Think about the apple trees again. The apple trees are also different," said his dad.

A *putt-putting* tractor pulling a flatbed trailer came down the road. It stopped in the yard near the wooden steps. Some people walked down the steps to get off the trailer, but most of them slid down over the edge to the ground.

One girl was inching her way past the bales of hay to the wooden steps. A boy was holding her hand. Tommy looked at the boy. It was Chris, the new boy in his class! Was the girl his sister?

Tommy saw his dad stand up and look at the crowd that had gathered for the next ride. Tommy stayed at his dad's side watching Chris and the girl.

"Dad," said Tommy, pulling on his dad's jacket, "that's Chris. He just moved here." Then he added quietly, "I didn't know he had a retarded sister."

The girl stared at the space between the edge of the trailer and the top step. She put out her foot toward the step, but she seemed scared to step over the space between the trailer and the step. She brought her foot back and looked up at Chris.

Someone should move the steps closer, thought Tommy. But no one seemed to notice the problem.

"Maybe I can push the steps closer," said Tommy to Dad. He walked over to the trailer, throwing his apple stick in a trash barrel.

"Hi, Chris," said Tommy. "Dad and I are going on the next ride."

"Hi, Tommy," said Chris. "I didn't know you were coming out here today."

Tommy tried to move the steps, but they were too heavy.

"Dad," called Tommy. "Could you help me move these steps?" Together they shoved the steps up to the trailer.

After the girl put both feet on the top step, she smiled down at Tommy. Continuing slowly, one step at a time, she came down the steps, her hand still tightly holding Chris's.

"This is my sister, Happy," said Chris, guiding her away from the steps so people could get on the trailer.

"Hi," said Tommy. "How was the ride?"

"Fun," said Happy.

"What did you see on the ride?" Tommy asked.

"Pretty apple trees," said Happy.

"We came with our neighbors," said Chris.

"Candy apple?" asked Happy, looking at her brother.

Chris said to Tommy. "I promised Happy an apple after the ride. The people we came with want to leave now. I don't have much time."

"I'll stay here with Happy while you get it," said Tommy.

"You'll miss your ride," said Chris.

"Maybe not," said Tommy, looking at some people still getting on the trailer.

Chris smiled at Tommy and said, "Thanks, I'll hurry."

Tommy grinned back.

A man started the tractor. Chris came back with two caramel apples. He handed one to Happy.

"Thanks for waiting with Happy, Tommy," said Chris. He took Happy's arm and led her across the gravel toward a parked car.

Tommy climbed up on the trailer and sat down on a bale of hay next to his dad. They turned around in the big farmyard and started down a narrow road. The graceful branches of white billowing blossoms surrounded them.

"Hello, and welcome to Sunnyside Orchard," said the man over a loud-speaker as he drove the tractor. "The blossoms are at their peak today. They're pink before they open all the way. I know you folks want sunny skies this summer, but the trees will need lots of rain in June, July, and August to give a good crop of apples."

The tractor pulled them along the bumpy road, up over a small hill and around a bend.

"The trees look alike," said the man, "but the apples they produce are different. We grow 27 different kinds."

Tommy looked at his dad and grinned. Dad winked at him.

"The trees you're passing now produce Delicious apples," the man went on. "They're an eating apple, good in the lunchbox. Don't bake them, though. They won't taste good."

The tractor wound through the trees.

"The apples from these trees you can bake in a pie or coffee cake. They're Cortlands," said the driver. "Apples are different colors and shapes. That helps us tell them apart. They taste different, too."

"People want to know what we do in winter," the man said. "We repair our machines, press cider and freeze it, and prune our trees. Pruning is a big job. We have 12,000 trees."

The man thanked the people for their visit. "Come back in September or October," he said. "We'll let you taste different kinds of apples so you can decide which kind you like before you buy a couple bushels." He chuckled.

"Can we come back and do that?" asked Tommy.

"Sure," said Dad, "I'd like to buy several kinds this fall."

The tractor headed back to the barn.

As they were driving home, Tommy's dad said, "That was nice of you to help Chris's sister."

"When the man told us how *apples* are different," said Tommy, "I thought about how *kids* are different. We talked about that in health class, too. It's OK to be different, because nobody's exactly like anyone else in the whole world. We learned how some kids are tall, some are short and things like that," said Tommy. "There are kids who don't learn very fast. Some kids are better at doing certain things than others. But if you're not good at one thing, like reading, you might be good at something else like swimming."

Then he said slowly, "I wonder why Chris's family calls his sister Happy. Maybe she's happy most of the time. Maybe she's good at being happy."

"You could be right," said Dad.

"I'll see her at Garfield School on Monday," said Tommy.

Come, O Children, Sing to Jesus

F. Smith

Come, O children, sing to Jesus
On this happy Easter Day.
"Christ, our Savior, now is risen,"
Let his little children say.

All the bells are gladly ringing,
All the flow'rs are gaily springing,
All the birds with joy are singing:
Come, dear children, praise and pray.

Pinney's Easter Hunt

Lavinia R. Davis

*I*t was Easter Sunday, but there was nothing very Eastery about the farm. The wind was cold and raw, the tan fields were still hard with frost, and only the maples in the south pasture were bright with red bud.

Pinney shivered as he pulled on his old wool jacket and went out to do the chores. You felt colder when you knew it was meant to be spring and still the world didn't warm up. It was always knowing about things that made them seem bad, like knowing about the Easter Hunt over at Wainbridge that very afternoon.

Pinney hurried up to the barn and tried not to think about the Easter Hunt, but that was impossible. You just couldn't help thinking about an egg hunt where they were going to give two live Bantam chickens to the boy who found the most eggs. Pinney waved to Grandpa and tried to chase away his thoughts. It wasn't Grandpa's fault that he had to milk all the cows and couldn't spare the time to drive all the way over to Wainbridge. And it wasn't Grundy's fault that she was just getting over the flu and couldn't drive Pinney over, either.

Pinney fed the chickens and the pigs. It certainly wasn't his grandparents' fault, but that didn't help. If only he hadn't known that there was even a chance of his winning a pair of Bantams he would have been better off.

When Pinney was all through with his chores, he suddenly had a good idea. Though the upper meadows were still frozen, it was much warmer

103

in the lowlands, and he might find some bloodroot or hepatica. He would transplant some into a little pot and give it to Grundy for an Easter plant. If somebody had an Easter surprise that afternoon Pinney thought he would feel better.

Pinney picked up a trowel and a basket in the woodshed and went into the woods. The twigs still snapped frostily under foot as they had in December, but at least now there were birds chirping, and as Pinney got near the swamp there were green pincushions of skunk cabbage to show that it wasn't midwinter.

After a little while Pinney dug his hands in his pockets and began to whistle. He hoped he would find the hepatica soon. He was cold and what he really wanted to do was to go home and read in front of the big pot-bellied stove. But he wanted to please Grundy, too, even if the March wind that cut in under his collar seemed colder and more unpleasant than any wind all winter.

Pinney kept on and on. He passed over Grandpa's boundary and walked onto Mr. Leggett's farm. Mr. Leggett was one of Pinney's friends and never minded his trespassing, but reaching his farm made Pinney realize how far he had gone from home. If he hadn't got any hepatica so far, there wouldn't be another chance until he got to the shelter of Leggett's ledge, which was right in the middle of the woodlot.

When he finally reached the ledge, Pinney's marching whistle suddenly quickened. Hepatica! Lots of it. Pale,

pale lavender flowers with a deep green leaf. Pinney looked around at the sheltering arms of the rock ledge approvingly. Nothing but the warm south wind could blow in here. It was a perfect, natural shelter.

Pinney picked out three good plants, dug them carefully, and placed them in his basket. They had good long roots so Grundy could transplant them later into her flower garden. He was just covering the roots when he heard the little noise behind him.

Baa, baa, baa. It was such a feeble little noise Pinney wasn't even sure he'd heard it. *Baa, baa,* the sound repeated, and Pinney shot around on his heel. For a second he didn't see anything and then, as its little black nose wriggled, he saw the lamb!

It was small, and woolly, and Pinney knew it must be very newly born! He patted its little round head and wondered why its mother had left it. Grandpa didn't raise sheep, and Pinney knew it was one of Mr. Leggett's flock. Perhaps Mr. Leggett or Jake MacTavish, his shepherd, had overlooked it. Except for its nose and its black stockinged legs, the lamb was a perfect match with the gray rock behind it. Even if the lamb had been overlooked, Pinney was sure someone would be back soon to carry it home.

He petted it for a moment, held it in his arms. It nestled close to him and trembled as if it needed his warmth. But Pinney put it down again. It stood uncertainly on its wobbly legs looking very forlorn. He mustn't get fond of it. It would probably be safe here, and

surely Jake would come back soon.

Pinney started picking up his trowel and basket, but he didn't feel like leaving. He wished Mr. Leggett or Jake would come back while he was there. He'd feel better if he saw them starting off with the lamb in their arms. Right now it looked awfully lonely and pathetic even in the shelter of the deep ledge.

Just before he started off, Pinney turned to have one more look at the lamb. It was much too weak to try to follow him. It lifted its little head, but even that took too much strength and it dropped against its woolly chest. Pinney tried to move. But then all of a sudden, he knew he couldn't leave the lamb.

He couldn't take a chance on Jake or Mr. Leggett not finding that lamb. He'd have to bring it home to them tonight. Even if the Leggett barn was

still a long, long walk away, Pinney knew he would have to get there. He just couldn't leave the lamb by itself.

Pinney picked it up in both arms, tucked it under his coat, and somehow gripped the basket in his fingertips. It was an awkward load, but Pinney was sure he could manage. He started his marching whistle again, only louder and quicker this time so that he would walk faster. He had a long way to go, and it was getting late. Left, right, left, right! Pinney went as fast as he could along the edge of the ledge, out of the protection of the woods, and across the windswept fields, up the long hill to the farmyard.

More than once he had to stop to repack his load. Either the lamb would move in his arms or the basket would slip in his stiff fingers. Then he would readjust his burdens, straighten his shoulders, and march on. It might have been safe to leave the lamb in the home field where Jake or Mr. Leggett would be sure to find it. It seemed safe. It probably was safe, but Pinney wasn't taking any chances. The little animal, nestling in his arms, was so small, so helpless. He spoke to it reassuringly and thought that it seemed to tremble less at his words.

Jake was milking when Pinney finally reached the barn. The place was warm and steamy with the breath of the feeding cows.

"Here's one of your lambs," Pinney said. "Found it by the ledge. Guess maybe it was lost." Carefully he unbuttoned his coat and displayed his small charge.

Jake took the lamb in his big gnarled hands. "Must be a twin to the black lambie the big ewe bore this morning," he said. "I brought home the blackie and couldna understand why the mother acted so strange at leaving the ledge."

Pinney nodded understandingly. He touched the lamb in farewell.

"Good night," he said and started for the door.

"Good night," Jake said still bending over the lamb. "You'll like be hearing from the master."

Pinney never even wondered what Jake could mean. There were other important things to think about. In the first place he had to run home to keep from being late, and in the second place Grundy and Grandpa were waiting for him anyhow. Besides he wanted to forget about the lamb. He was glad that it was safe.

Grundy was up and about for the first time in a week and all dressed in her best blue silk that always meant a party. Grandpa was all through milking and was already fussing about the kitchen making flapjacks, which were his own particular specialty for birthdays and Christmas and Easter.

Pinney potted his plants in red pots he found in the cellar. He gave them to Grundy as they sat down to their supper. She hugged him and thanked him just as if he'd brought her three dozen store roses all for herself. Finally she gave him another hug and nodded to Pinney's own place. There were two very specially handpainted eggs that Grundy had dyed for Pinney herself. Then there was a chocolate rabbit that Grandpa had bought at the store and a shiny new nickel lay beside it.

Pinney said his thanks and as he poured syrup on Grandpa's flapjacks, he promised himself he wouldn't ever think about the Wainbridge egg hunt and the Bantams again.

But it was an easier promise to make than to keep. The very next morning he woke up with an empty disappointed sort of feeling hanging all over him.

Resolutely he jumped out of bed and pulled on his clothes. He wasn't going to think about it. He really wasn't.

He hadn't even started his breakfast before Grundy called to him. "Been up to the barn yet, sonny?" she asked, and her voice sounded as mysterious as Santa Claus. "Been up to the barn yet to feed the pigs?"

When Pinney was all through his oatmeal and his fried eggs and bacon, he went up to the barn. Grandpa was tinkering with the tractor in the shed, but when he saw Pinney, he dropped his tools. "Been over to the barn yet?" he asked, and he, too, sounded mysterious.

Once Pinney was inside the barn he understood. There, right in front of him, was the little lamb he'd returned to the Leggetts yesterday!

The lamb's little black nose was the same. Its black stockinged legs were the same. Its round tennis ball head was the same. It just looked a little stronger, and around its neck on a piece of green raffia hung an envelope. Pinney went nearer and saw his name on the outside.

He pulled it open and looked inside. "Happy Easter," he read. "And good luck. See if you can bring this lamb up as well as you brought him home."

"He's yours to keep," Grandpa said. "Tom Leggett brought him over this morning. Said any boy who had the gumption to take so much trouble to bring a lamb home ought to own one. He brought along a nursing bottle for you to feed him with."

For a long time Pinney couldn't say anything. He just hugged the lamb and thought how it made a better pet than even the finest Bantams.

The lamb tried to lick his hands, and then suddenly Pinney spoke. "Just think! Suppose I'd gone to Wainbridge and nobody had found the lamb!"

I Am Jesus' Little Lamb

Henrietta L. Von Hayn

I am Jesus' little lamb,
Ever glad at heart I am;
For my Shepherd gently guides me,
Knows my need and well provides me.
Loves me ev'ry day the same,
Even calls me by my name.

Empty Places

Betty Lou Mell

Tippie died on a Wednesday afternoon. In all other ways, it was a normal, uneventful day. Jessica rushed home from school, as always, but instead of seeing her mother, she saw a note: "Jessi, something is wrong with Tippie. Your father came home from work to take her and Mrs. Rupert to the vet. Be back soon. Love, Mom."

Jessica let Major outside and read the note again. It must be serious for Dad to leave work, she thought. She let Major back in, then patted his head and sat at the kitchen table. "Please, dear God," she prayed, "Tippie is all Mrs. Rupert has, please don't let anything happen to her."

She was looking out the window when she saw the car pull into the driveway. She rushed to the door. Dad was helping Mrs. Rupert with the cat carrier. Her mother came around the car and put her arm around Jessica's shoulders. From the look on everyone's faces, Jessica knew.

"I'll take care of Tippie for you," Dad offered.

Jessica watched as Mrs. Rupert wiped her eyes with a tissue, then forced a smile. "You've done enough already, Craig, this is something I have to do myself."

Jessica struggled with her own tears as Mrs. Rupert walked across the lawn to her house. Finally, Jessica asked, "What happened?"

Her father shook his head. "Tippie had a heart attack," he said. Then he kissed mother and hugged Jessica. "Don't cook, Ann," he said as he turned to the car. "I'll pick up something for us on my way home from work."

Jessica's mother took her hand. "Tippie was such a nice cat, I'll miss her too."

Jessica sat on the windowseat looking at Mrs. Rupert's house while Major sprawled at her feet. She tried to imagine life without Major. Who would climb onto Dad's favorite chair, or bark at strangers, or wake her with rough-tongued kisses? She thought of Mrs. Rupert and tried to imagine her working in her yard without Tippie purring around her feet.

Then she saw Mrs. Rupert walking toward the back of her yard. In her hands was the cat carrier. Jessica watched as Mrs. Rupert put the carrier gently on the ground under the elm tree, then go to the garage. When she came out, she carried a shovel.

A week passed in which forsythia bloomed and tulips unfolded. But Jessica only saw Mrs. Rupert out twice, and each time she looked sad and lonely. Jessica even caught herself looking for Tippie at Mrs. Rupert's window when she came home from school—before she remembered.

Finally at dinner one night, Jessica said, "You know how you always tell me God provides everything?"

Dad nodded. "He does."

"Well," Jessica continued thoughtfully. "Will he fill the empty place in Mrs. Rupert's life—I mean, the place Tippie used to fill?"

Father blinked. "Everything belongs to God, honey, so everything we have comes from God in one way or another. But sometimes God wants us to fill empty places ourselves."

Jessica leaned forward. "How do you mean?"

"When we know someone needs something, we should do what we can to help," he explained.

"We should?" Jessica asked eagerly.

Father nodded. "Yes."

"How do you know you're doing the right thing?"

Mother smiled curiously. "You can usually tell by how you feel. What are you thinking about, honey?"

Jessica shrugged. "I'd like to get Mrs. Rupert another kitten."

Father took a deep breath. "She was so close to Tippie, honey. . . ."

"You can tell by the way she looks," Jessica replied quickly, "that another kitten would be better than none."

Father nodded. "Yes, but. . . ."

Mother reached across the table for his hand. "Jessi may be right," she said.

Jessica smiled instantly. "And I already picked out another kitten for her," she said quickly.

Her mother and father looked at her in surprise. "You did?"

Jessica nodded. "On my way from school, I stopped at the Animal Rescue League. There's a kitten with all its shots, and I have enough money to pay for it. But I need an adult to sign for it. Will you sign, please?"

They laughed. "We'll sign," her father said, "and we'll pay for it too."

Jessica cupped the tiny kitten in one hand and knocked at Mrs. Rupert's door. Beside her, Major wagged his tail and panted. When Mrs. Rupert opened her door, she smiled at them.

"Jessica, what a darling little kitten!" she exclaimed. "May I hold him?"

"It's a her," Jessica replied.

Mrs. Rupert held the kitten high in her hands and looked in its face. "She's adorable! What are you going to name her?"

"She's yours," Jessica said. "So it's up to you to name her."

Mrs. Rupert stared. "Mine?"

"We got her at the Animal Rescue League. Here's some kitten food. They give it to you free."

Mrs. Rupert's eyes were watery. "Come in, honey—you and Major," she said happily.

Jessica followed her to the kitchen and watched as she filled two saucers with milk. As the kitten lapped one, Major gulped the other, then stared at the kitten's saucer longingly. Mrs. Rupert looked up and laughed. "I don't know what to say, except, thank you. I thought about another kitten, but. . . ."

The kitten left the saucer and bounded around the table legs, then flopped on her back at Mrs. Rupert's feet. Major moved to the kitten's milk, and the kitten flicked a playful paw at Major's wagging tail. Then it tore off to peek around the corner. "She reminds me of Tippie, when she was a kitten," Mrs. Rupert said. "But what made you think of getting me another cat?"

Jessica shrugged. She couldn't put it into words.

Mrs. Rupert smiled and hugged Jessica lightly. "That's called caring," she said quietly.

Stepka and the Magic Fire

A Russian Easter Legend
Retold by Dorothy Van Woerkom

In the days of the Tsars, on a hill above the Don River, was a certain poor village. No one in the village had very much in those days.

The wars of Tsar Ivan the Terrible had ruined nearly all of Russia. The land had failed and the harvests were bad. Towns could no longer pay their taxes. Roaming bands of Cossacks frightened the peasants, and stole from them.

But the family of Stepka had least of all. Stepka and his three small daughters lived on brown bread and water from the New Year to the Nativity.

Still, when Easter arrived on the high winds of late March, the village people tried to make the best of it. On Easter Eve they brought out precious sacks of flour for cakes and cookies. They ate cabbage soup and salted cucumber and tea with lemon in it. After dark they lit their homes with Easter candles. And in every house but Stepka's there was fire against the cold March wind.

At midnight neighbors ran from house to house. They carried torches to light their way. They wore bright smiles above their feast-day clothes. With shouts and laughter they called the Easter greeting to each other.

"Christ is risen!" they cried. And, "He is risen indeed!"

Stepka did not join the others. He put his hungry children to bed with a song on his lips, with a pain in his heart. Long after they had fallen asleep he watched them as they lay huddled together on their cot. Tomorrow's breakfast would be more brown bread. But tomorrow was Easter!

For Easter, at least, they should have something special.

From a cupboard Stepka took a box of old Easter candles. He counted them out on the table. He longed to place them about the house and light them, to wake the children and watch their faces glow with pleasure. Only there was no fire in his house with which to light them. And he had no wood to make one.

Now Stepka was a man too proud to beg. But just this once—for the children—he would do it. He hurried down the hill and through the village to beg some fire from his neighbors.

"Give me a light for my Easter candles, good neighbor," he cried again and again. "A light for the love of heaven!"

"Be gone!" they told him.

"Take better care of your affairs, neighbor," they shouted.

"See the bright moon above?" they mocked. "Get a good long stick and take as much light as you need!"

And all the while to each other they were saying, "Christ is risen!" And, "He is risen indeed!"

Stepka turned his back on them. He plodded slowly up the cobbled street toward his home. His shoulders drooped. His stomach was as empty as his pockets. Cold and hunger made him dizzy.

That was why he thought he must be seeing things when the row of fires appeared below him on the plain. He rubbed his eyes and looked again. Cossacks! He hurried to get home before they attacked the village.

But, wait! These fires had a certain look to them; they must belong to a band of charcoal-burners camping on the plain. Stepka scrambled down the

hill to ask them for a light. Could they treat him worse than his own neighbors had?

The nearer he came to the camp, the brighter burned the fires. Just the sight of them warmed him. The coming and going of people around the flames cheered him onward. The laughter and the calling of one to another made him feel welcome, even though he knew they had not yet seen him.

Stepka walked right up to the nearest fire. He swept off his cap and cried, "Christ is risen!"

"He is risen indeed!" replied one of the men at the fire.

Now, this is a proper greeting, thought Stepka. And so: "Give me a light for my Easter candles, good people, I pray you."

"Help yourself, and welcome." The charcoal-burner's smile made cracks in the layers of soot around his mouth and eyes.

Stepka reached for the shovel which the stranger held out to him. Then he stopped and stared at his hands. Now that he could have his fire, he had nothing in which to carry it.

"Oh!" Stepka struck his forehead with the heel of his hand. "I never thought to bring my charcoal pot."

"Well, my friend," said the charcoal-burner, "You were anxious for your family. A man who worries does not always have his head on straight." He laughed and pushed the shovel into the fire. "But we can right that soon enough. Spread your coat out over there."

Stepka pulled off his old patched coat and laid it near the fire. His amazement turned to anger as the fellow threw two shovelfuls of blazing wood onto the coat.

"Hallo! Hallo!" Stepka seized his arm. "What are you about, man, to burn my coat this way?"

"Your coat is none the worse for it, my friend," the charcoal-burner told him. "Look and see."

Stepka looked. The fire lay quietly in the hollow of the coat. It never singed a thread of it. Stepka was too surprised to move.

"Good luck to you, my friend." The charcoal-burner stooped to gather up the coat. He handed it to Stepka. "You will have no trouble getting it home. Trust me."

Like a man in a dream, Stepka climbed back up the hill. From time to time he stopped to stare into the glowing wood. He held the coat closer to his face to feel the warmth. It was not to be believed. Yet it was true!

He pushed open the door of his cold dark house. He set the coat gently on the scratched top of the wooden table. With fingers that trembled he lighted first one candle, then another. The last candle flickered as if it would die. Then it glowed as bravely as the others. Stepka sighed.

Softly he called to the children. They would still be hungry, but they would have their Easter lights. Their smiles were his reward. They laughed and clapped their hands and threw their arms around him. His surprise had made them forget their hunger.

But in this night of surprises there was yet another surprise for Stepka. One of the children pointed to his coat on the table and shouted.

The coat was full of gold coins!

Stepka hurried over. He took the gold and let it slip through his fingers: more coins than he could count in an hour! He gathered the children to him and fell on his knees. He wept and prayed and laughed and wept some more.

Outside the little house, neighbors passing by had seen the lights and heard the laughter.

"What have *they* to be merry about?" one of them asked, peering through a window. He saw the heap of gold on the table. He whirled around to the door and shoved it open.

"I say!" demanded this neighbor of Stepka's. He did not take time for the feast-day greeting, "Christ is risen." "Where did you get such a fine fortune? My eyes want to blink at the sight of it!"

Stepka was not a man who bore a grudge or sought revenge. He told his neighbor of his visit to the charcoal-burners.

One moment the neighbor was standing in front of Stepka, the next he was dashing down the hill. Other villagers, who had crowded into the open doorway to listen, hurried after him. They had not even reached the plain before the whole village came following.

The leader of the charcoal-burners lifted his blackened eyebrows. He was surprised to see so many coming all at once to beg a light. He said nothing, however, except that they should spread their coats on the ground. He motioned for his followers to heap two shovelfuls of burning wood into the hollow of each coat.

Up the hill sped the greedy villagers. They crowed to themselves over such easy riches. They told each other how they planned to spend their money.

Suddenly a cry rang out. Another, and another. The fire was burning through their heavy coats! Sparks and ashes spilled down their feast-day clothes. Blisters stung their hands.

All that was left of their riches was a smoke and a smell like the burning of fifty tar-barrels.

They turned back to shake their fists at the charcoal-burners. Then they stood with their mouths open. Their groans of pain, their shouts of anger, became cries of astonishment.

The strangers were gone. The fires had disappeared. The plain stretched out below, covered with grass and brush. Nothing more.

The villagers were sore and sorry, but Stepka kept his gold. He became the richest man for miles around. Yet his money did not make a selfish man of him. His door was always open to the poor. And every year, on Easter Eve, he walked up and down along the river. He called to poor folk, one and all, to come and share his Easter meal.

When he died, his grandson, also called Stepka, did the same and Stepka his great-grandson as well. That was how, in time, the little village because known as Stepkov. And that was how Stepkov became the most famous village on the Don.

On This Blessed Easter Day

On this blessed Easter day
Little children sing
Joyful song of love and praise
Unto Christ the King.

Of Course It's Spring
Alan Cliburn

Debbie Malone frowned as she sat in the car waiting for her mother. She stared up at the big apartment building where they lived. At first she had liked living in the city, so high up that people looked like dolls walking along the sidewalk below.

But she didn't like it anymore. The newspaper said it was spring, the warmer weather said it was spring, even her mother and father said it was spring. But it wasn't spring to Debbie. Spring meant pretty flowers growing in the garden.

There were no gardens and no flowers in the city, except in the park, many blocks away.

Mrs. Malone came out of the building. "My, what a lovely spring morning!"

"I don't think it's really spring," Debbie said.

"The snow has melted and the sky is blue," her mother replied. "Of course it's spring!"

"I don't see any flowers," Debbie said.

"You will," Mrs. Malone promised. "We have to stop at Mr. Watson's pet store for bird seed. He always has flowers in the window."

Debbie smiled. She liked going to Mr. Watson's store. Still, flowers in the window weren't the same as flowers growing in a garden.

"Well, hello Debbie," Mr. Watson said. "Is your parakeet all out of food again?"

"Almost," Debbie told him. She went over to smell the flowers. "Maybe it is spring," she said slowly.

"Of course it's spring!" Mr. Watson agreed with a laugh. "Here's your bird seed."

Her mother paid for the seed and they started to leave. Then Debbie stopped. "Mr. Watson, why did you throw away all these seeds?" They were in a wastebasket near the door.

Mr. Watson shook his head. "They were brought here by mistake. They aren't even bird seed, they're flower seeds! All different kinds mixed together. No one around here wants flower seeds, so I just threw them out."

"Can I have them?" Debbie wanted to know.

"Debbie, what would you do with flower seeds?" her mother asked. "We don't have any space for a garden; we live in an apartment."

"I know," Debbie said, "but can't I take them anyway? I'll think of something to do with them."

"It's all right with me," Mr. Watson told her with a smile. "I'll put them in a sack for you."

114

"Thank you," Debbie said.

Mrs. Malone was quiet as they drove home. "You miss the flower garden we had at our old house, don't you?" she asked finally.

"Yes," Debbie replied. "That's why I wanted the flower seeds. Maybe I can have my own little garden here in the city!"

"But how?" her mother questioned. "Where?"

"I'll get some dirt and sand at the park," Debbie explained. "And I'll plant the seeds in those old flower pots I saw in the basement of our apartment building. I'll keep them in my room."

"But flowers need sunlight and air," Mrs. Malone reminded her. "I'm afraid they wouldn't grow in your room."

"Then I'll put them on the window sill," Debbie said. "They won't fall because of the railing."

"OK," her mother agreed. "But you'll have to take care of them."

"I'll do everything myself," Debbie promised. "You'll see, in a few weeks we'll have flowers everywhere and it'll really be spring!"

First Debbie asked the manager if she could use the flower pots stored in the basement.

"Sure, and I'll even bring them up to your apartment," he said. "How many do you want?"

"All of them," Debbie answered. "I have lots of seeds."

Next Debbie took a big bucket, put it on a wagon borrowed from a boy down the hall and went to the park.

"We just got some fresh dirt and sand," the gardener told her. "Take as much as you need."

Carefully Debbie pulled the wagon back along the sidewalk, the bucket full to the very top. She pulled it right into the elevator and went up to the eighth floor.

"Debbie, the manager sent up 20 pots!" Mrs. Malone exclaimed. "Did you want so many?"

"Oh, yes!" Debbie said.

There was just enough dirt and sand for all 20 flower pots. Next Debbie took the sack Mr. Watson had given her and planted a few seeds in each pot. After that she placed all the pots on the window sill.

"You've been working most of the afternoon," her mother said. "Aren't you through yet?"

"Almost," Debbie replied. "I have to water them, then I'll be finished."

"Don't expect them to grow overnight," Mrs. Malone warned. "Flowers take time."

"I know," Debbie smiled. "But I can wait. And if I take very good care of them, maybe I won't have to wait as long."

Every day when she came home from school, Debbie checked her flower pots and watered each one. The first few days nothing happened. Not even a tiny green sprout appeared.

"Why are all those flower pots in your window?" Mr. Brockman asked her one day. He lived in the next apartment.

"I want it to be spring," Debbie explained. "I've planted flower seeds."

"Ridiculous!" Mr. Brockman told her. "It's already spring! And you'll never grow garden flowers inside."

Debbie looked at the flower pots later. Nothing was growing.

But she kept watering them every day. Sometimes Mr. Brockman looked out his window while she was working and shook his head. Debbie just smiled and went right on with her watering.

She didn't really feel like smiling, though. Maybe Mr. Brockman was right about growing flowers in those old pots. It would be silly to pour water on something that would never grow. But she wasn't quite ready to give up, not yet.

One morning Debbie stepped to the window for some fresh air. Her mouth dropped open in surprise. There in one of the pots was a small green shoot, just barely sticking up. She looked in the other pots. There was another and another!

By the time she returned home from school, almost every pot had tiny bits of green coming out of the soil. She was very careful with her watering.

"Weeds!" Mr. Brockman said. "That's what they look like to me!"

A few weeks later, the "weeds" were in full bloom, showing off their blues and yellows and pinks and violets.

"They're beautiful!" Debbie cried. "It really is spring, after all—even in the city!"

"Of course it's spring," her mother said. "And your flowers are lovely. They make our apartment look like a garden."

"When I'm coming home from work I can tell which apartment is ours two blocks away," Mr. Malone told Debbie. "It's the only one with flowers in the window."

"The only one?" Debbie repeated. She frowned. It didn't seem fair to have all the flowers, even if she had grown them herself.

"I think I'll give some of my flowers to the neighbors," she said. "I want everyone to know it's spring. Especially Mr. Brockman!"

Prayers

Holy Week
Pat Corrick Hinton

Loving Father,
during these holy days
we ask you for the gift
to understand
the dying and rising
of your Son Jesus.

Change our hearts
and our attitudes
so that as we die with him
to all that keeps us
from you
we will surely live with him
in your love and glory
forever.

Amen.

Wondering
Pat Corrick Hinton

Lord Jesus,
you taught us
how to trust
by the way you prayed
in the garden
before you died.

You knew
some terrible things
were going to happen
to you.
You must have wondered
how you would be able
to stand it.
You even asked the Father
to take it away.

You simply told him
exactly how you felt,
and through this prayer
you were able to accept his will
for you.

Teach us how to do this.
Help us to turn our dread
of what will happen
into trust
in the Father's love.

Show us that our prayer
can be a willingness to accept
what is going to happen.

It Was for Me!
Lois Walfrid Johnson

Jesus,
sometimes your death
on the cross
seems far away.
Then I remember
that it wasn't
just for my mom,
and dad,
or my friends
that you died.
It was for
me,
me,
me!
And then
your suffering
and your forgiveness
are real.
Thank you
for taking my place.

Jesus Lives!
Chris Jones

Thank you Lord, for coming to earth,
for making people happy,
for making them well,
for teaching about God
and for dying on the cross.
But most of all, thank you
for coming alive again.
Now we can go to heaven
because you paid for our sins.
Thank you for that, Lord Jesus.

All Glory, Laud, and Honor
Theodulph of Orleans
Translated by John M. Neale

All glory, laud, and honor
To you, redeemer, king,
To whom the lips of children
Made sweet hosannas ring.

You are the king of Israel
And David's royal Son,
Now in the Lord's name coming,
Our King and Blessed One.

Their praises you accepted;
Accept the prayers we bring,
Great author of all goodness,
O good and gracious King.

All glory, laud, and honor
To you, redeemer, king,
To whom the lips of children
Made sweet hosannas ring.

Easter Is a Good Time
Ron and Lyn Klug

Easter is a good time, Jesus,
because we remember
that you died for us
and became alive again.
Thank you for living with us always.

For Special Days
Judith Mattison

Easter—
sunshine, fresh air,
dew glistening on the grass
Easter—
not eggs and candy
but a colorful celebration
of the chance Jesus gave me
to start over again.
Easter means he will
forgive any mistakes
and give me new life—
every day.
Easter is happy
because Easter is always new,
always fresh.
I never have to give up
because Jesus never stopped living
and never stops loving me.
Happy Easter!

Lord, Bless Everything!
Ron and Lyn Klug

Lord, bless everything that grows:
flowers and grass and trees,
tadpoles and caterpillars,
baby birds and small fuzzy animals,
and me!

Easter
Pat Corrick Hinton

There's something new
and wonderful today, Lord,
something in the air.

It's an excitement
and a tingling
and a feeling we'll explode
with joy.

For you have truly risen, Lord.
The Father has gifted
all the world
with your new life.

And we share in it.

Thank you for the wonder of it all.

You Are Alive!
Lois Walfrid Johnson

So often I don't stop to think
about Easter's real meaning.
I need to jump out of bed,
run to the garden,
hear for myself
the angel saying,
"He has risen, he is not here!"
Surprise me, Lord!
Fill me with the joy
of that early morning,
so that I understand
what it means for me
that you are
alive!
alive!
alive!

Prayer After Nine Rainy Days (or Two or Three)
Pat Corrick Hinton

Loving Father,
we know
the rain you send
is a gift,
and we thank you.

We know our grass and plants
were very dry.
We know all your creatures
need water.

But all this rain
gets a little boring.

We're tired of being inside
or getting soaked
when we go outside.

Show us your sunshine
soon, Father.
And help us wait.
Amen.

Prayer on a Spring Day
Pat Corrick Hinton

Father,
thank you for making
the whole world
come alive again
after the long winter.

Thank you for the joy
I felt today
when I saw flowers
about to open.

Each blue and white and yellow
and red flower
is a gift from you.

Thank you for showing
your love
through the beautiful things
you have made.

Amen.

It Smells So Good!
Chris Jones

It smells so good outside today.
The snow's almost gone,
and the grass is squishy, wet, and muddy.
Now I can catch frogs and small silver fish
and splash in the puddles
when the rain has stopped.
Now I can play baseball again.
Thank you, God, for springtime,
when everything turns from black and white
to green and yellow
and all my friends are out on their bikes again.

Carols

Hosanna

Sharon Dale

Sharon Dale

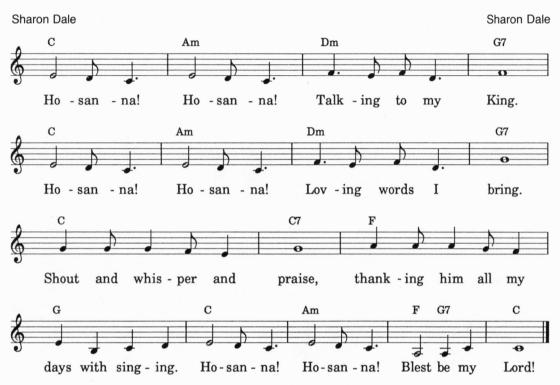

Ho - san - na! Ho - san - na! Talk - ing to my King.

Ho - san - na! Ho - san - na! Lov - ing words I bring.

Shout and whis - per and praise, thank - ing him all my

days with sing - ing. Ho - san - na! Ho - san - na! Blest be my Lord!

Christ the Lord Is Ris'n Today

Author Unknown

Robert Williams

1. Christ the Lord is ris'n to - day: Al - le - lu - ia!
2. Chris - tians, praise the Lord and say: Al - le - lu - ia!

Oh, God Didn't Give Me Much

Judy Thompson Beyers

Judy Thompson Beyers

1. Oh, God did-n't give me much, just the sun-light in the
2. Oh, God did-n't give me much, just the green leaves of
3. Oh, God did-n't give me much, just the breath that I'm
4. Oh, God did-n't give me much, just a Son that died

morn - ing, just the moon - light at night, just a
sum - mer, just the gold leaves of fall, just the
breath - ing, just the heart that beats strong, just a
for me, just an end to my strife, just a

breeze through my win - dow, just a warm sum - mer night.
white snow of win - ter, just a lit - tle bird's call.
warm touch of friend - ship, just the sign I be - long.
home up in heav - en, just the prom - ise of life.

It's a Happy Day

Gary Pfieffer

Gary Pfieffer

It's a hap-py day, and I thank God for the weath - er.

— It's a hap-py day, and I'm liv - in' it for my Lord.

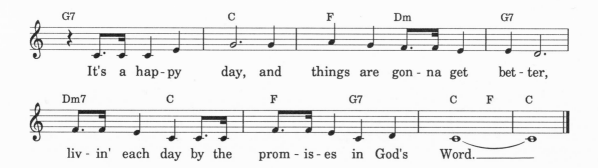

It's a hap-py day, and things are gon-na get bet-ter,
liv-in' each day by the prom-is-es in God's Word.____

On This Blessed Easter Day

Traditional   Traditional

Oh, how joy-ful-ly,____ oh, how mer-ri-ly____

church bells ring on this East-er Day!

Christ the Lord is ris-en from the grave's dark pris-on

on this hap-py, on this bless-ed East-er Day!

Jesus, My Lord and God

Ron Klug

John Ferguson

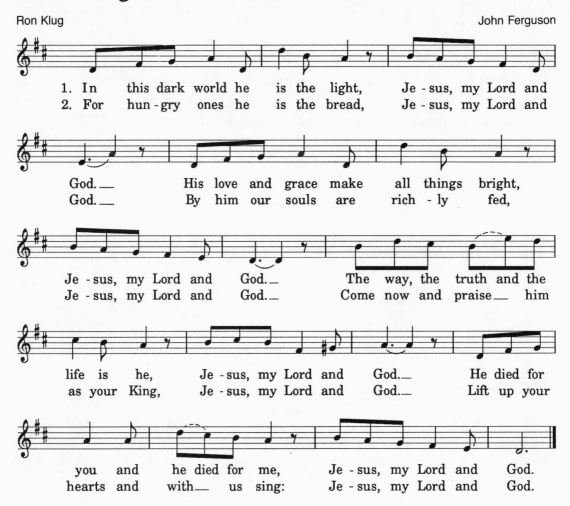

1. In this dark world he is the light, Je-sus, my Lord and
2. For hun-gry ones he is the bread, Je-sus, my Lord and

God. — His love and grace make all things bright,
God. — By him our souls are rich-ly fed,

Je-sus, my Lord and God. — The way, the truth and the
Je-sus, my Lord and God. — Come now and praise— him

life is he, Je-sus, my Lord and God. — He died for
as your King, Je-sus, my Lord and God. — Lift up your

you and he died for me, Je-sus, my Lord and God.
hearts and with— us sing: Je-sus, my Lord and God.

Beautiful Savior

Gesangbuch, tr. Joseph A. Seiss

Silesian Folk Tune

1. Beau - ti - ful Sav - ior, King of cre - a - tion,
2. Fair are the mead - ows, fair are the wood - lands,
3. Fair is the sun - shine, fair is the moon - light,
4. Beau - ti - ful Sav - ior, Lord of the na - tions,

Son of God and Son of Man!
robed in flow'rs of bloom - ing spring;
bright the spar - kling stars on high;
Son of God and Son of Man!

Tru - ly I'd love thee, tru - ly I'd serve thee,
Je - sus is fair - er, Je - sus is pur - er,
Je - sus shines bright - er, Je - sus shines pur - er
Glo - ry and hon - or, praise, ad - o - ra - tion,

Light of my soul, my joy, my crown.
he makes our sor - r'wing spir - it sing.
than all the an - gels in the sky.
now and for - ev - er more be thine!

The King of Glory

Willard F. Jabusch

Israeli Folk Tune

Refrain

The King of glo-ry comes; the na-tion re - joic - es.

O -pen the gates be -fore him, lift up your voic - es.

Fine

1. Who is the King of glo - ry; how shall we call him?
2. He gave his life for us, the pledge of sal - va - tion,
3. He con -quered sin and death; he tru - ly has ris - en.

He is Em - man - u - el, the prom -ised of a - ges.
and took up - on him - self the sins of the na - tion.
And he will share with us his heav - en - ly vi - sion.

Refrain

Acknowledgments

Every effort has been made to trace the ownership of all copyrighted material and to secure the permissions necessary to reprint these selections. Any error or oversight will be corrected in future printings if such omission is made known.

9   Copyright © 1989 Augsburg Fortress.
14 Used by permission of Cass R. Sandak.
19 "Easter Day, Glad Easter Day." From *Little Children, Sing to God!*, copyright © 1960 Concordia Publishing House. Used by permission.
19 "Todd's Search for Spring." Used by permission of Margaret Springer.
22 Used by permission of Alice Sullivan Finlay.
24 First published in the April 1980 issue of *The Friend*. Used by permission of Paula DePaolo.
27 From *Easter in Poetry*, copyright © 1926 H. W. Wilson Company. Used by permission.
31 From *Highlights for Children* (Columbus, Ohio), copyright © 1939. Used by permission.
34 Used by permission of Friends General Conference (FGC), 1520-B Race Street, Philadelphia, PA 19102. All rights reserved.
36 Used by permission of Joyce Nelms.
39 Used by permission of Marcella Fischer Anderson.
42 From *In My Nursery* by Laura Elizabeth Richards (Boston: Little, Brown and Company).
43 Used by permission of Margaret D. Wollington.
47 Used by permission of Marjorie Ellert Berg.
50 From *Pancakes and Painted Eggs* by Jean Chapman, Hodder & Stoughton Australia Pty Ltd, 1981. Used by permission.
51 From *Twelve Months Make a Year* by Elizabeth Coatsworth, copyright © 1943 Macmillan Publishing Company, renewed 1971 Elizabeth Coatsworth Beston. Used by permission of Macmillan Publishing Company.
52 "Spring in the Woods." Used by permission of Sandra Liatsos.
52 "An Easter Lily for Grandma." Used by permission of Mabel N. McCaw.
54 Used by permission of Linell Wohlers.
56 Used by permission of Gay Bell.
58 From *Friend in Strange Garments* by Anna Milo Upjohn, copyright © 1927 The American National Red Cross. Used by permission of Houghton Mifflin Company.
61 Used by permission of Helen Mallmann.
64 Used by permission of Majorie Hillert.
65 Used by permission of Alan Cliburn.
68 Used by permission of Margaret Shauers.
69 Copyright © 1989 Augsburg Fortress.
74 "Let's Celebrate." Used by permission of Jacqueline Rowland.
74 "The Easter Basket." Used by permission of Sandra Liatsos.
75 Used by permission of Denise J. Williamson.
77 Used by permission of Laurel Dee Gugler.
78 Used by permission of Laurel Dee Gugler.
80 From *The Wonder Garden* by Frances Jenkins Olcott, copyright © 1919, 1947 Frances Jenkins Olcott. Used by permission of Houghten Mifflin Company.
82 "I'm a Garden Helper." Used by permission of Shirley Pope Waite.
82 "Puddles." Used by permission of Donna Lugg Pape.
83 First published in the April 1961 issue of *The Children's Friend*. Used by permission of Martha Tolles.
84 Used by permission of Lucille Ellison.
85 Used by permission of Nora C. Hunter and David R. Brink.
87 Used by permission of Frances Carfi Matranga.
90 Used by permission of Brigid Casey-Meyer.
93 Used by permission of Martha Tolles.
94 From *Elena Pappas Is My Best Friend*, copyright © 1986 Phyllis Yingling. Used by permission of Julian Messner, a division of Simon and Schuster, Inc.
96 Used by permission of Jacqueline Rowland.

97 Used by permission of Wendy Pfeffer.
98 Used by permission of Gay Bell.
99 Used by permission of Helen Mallmann.
103 "Come, O Children, Sing to Jesus." *From Little Children, Sing to God!,* copyright © 1960 Concordia Publishing House. Used by permission.
103 "Pinney's Easter Hunt" Copyright © Lavinia R. Davis. Used by permission of Samuel S. Walker Jr., executive of the Lavina R. Davis Estate.
108 Used by permission of Betty Lou Mell.
110 Used by permission of Dorothy Van Woerkom.
113 From *A Child's Garden of Song,* copyright © 1945 Concordia Publishing House. Used by permission.
114 First published in the *American Junior Red Cross News.* Used by permission of Alan Cliburn.
117 "Holy Week" and "Wandering." From *Prayers for Growing and Other Pains,* copyright © 1981 Pat Corrick Hinton. Used by permission.
118 "It Was for Me!" From *Just a Minute, Lord* by Lois Walfrid Johnson, copyright © 1973 Augsburg Publishing House.
118 "Jesus Lives!" From *Lord, I Want to Tell You Something* by Chris Jones, copyright © 1973 Augsburg Publishing House.
118 "Easter Is a Good Time." From *Thank you, Lord* by Ron and Lyn Klug, copyright © 1980 Augsburg Publishing House.
119 "For Special Days" (first published as "Easter"). From *Who Will Listen to Me?* by Judith Mattison copyright © 1977 Augsburg Publishing House.
119 "Lord, Bless Everything!" From *Please, God* by Ron and Lyn Klug, copyright © 1980 Augsburg Publishing House.
119 "Easter." From *Prayers for Growing and Other Pains,* copyright © 1981 Pat Corrick Hinton. Used by permission.
119 "You Are Alive!" From *Just a Minute, Lord* by Lois Walfrid Johnson, copyright © 1973 Augsburg Publishing House.
120 "Prayer after Nine Rainy Days" and "Prayer on a Spring Day." Used by Permission of Pat Corrick Hinton.
120 "It Smells So Good!" From *Lord, I Want to Tell You Something* by Chris Jones, copyright © 1973 Augsburg Publishing House.
121 "Hosanna" from *Hosanna Vacation Bible School Songbook,* copyright © 1977 Augsburg Publishing House.
122 "Oh, God Didn't Give Me Much." Copyright © Judy Thompson Beyers. Used by permission.
122 "It's a Happy Day." Copyright © 1973 Fred Bock Music Company. All rights reserved. Used by permission.
123 From *A Child's Garden of Song,* copyright © 1945 Concordia Publishing House. Used by permission.
124 Reprinted from the anthem arrangement of "Jesus, My Lord and God " by John Ferguson and Ronald Klug, copyright © 1984 Augsburg Publishing House.
126 "The King of Glory." Copyright © 1966 Willard F. Jabusch, University of St. Mary of the Lake, Mundelein Seminary, Mundelein, IL 60060. Used by permission.